CW00554178

CONTENTS

VICARS

1921 – 1958   Alfred Hope Patten

1959 – 1976   Alan Arthur Roe

1977 – 1989   John Edgar Barnes

1989 – 1995   Michael John Rear

1995 – 1999   Keith Frank Michael Haydon

2000 – 2011   Norman Aidan Banks

2013 – 2018   Andrew Mark Mitcham

2018   Harri Alan McClelland Williams*

(* The Living was suspended in 2018, however Fr Harri was Inducted as the Vicar of the Benefice on 6th May 2021)

FOREWORD

The Rt Revd and Rt Hon The Lord Hope of Thornes KCVO, PC

*Sometime Archbishop of York and Master of the Guardians
of the Shrine of Our Lady of Walsingham*

The portraits of former incumbents are often to be seen hanging on the walls of the vestries of parish churches up and down the land. Whether they act as an encouragement or dissuasion to the current holder of that office can be a matter of opinion – some of them look quite threatening, one or two encouraging, some pretty vacuous, most of them quite serious and without any expression at all. In my former home at Bishopthorpe I was surrounded by my predecessors. They were there in the morning as I made my way to the chapel, they were there when I went out and when I came in – they seemed to follow me everywhere. For the most part their general demeanour seemed to be a resigned boredom.

Boredom is not an epithet that could ever be attached to William Davage's profiles of successive parish priests of Walsingham from the charismatic Fr Hope Patten to the present day. In many ways it could be said that Walsingham and its parish church were but one of so many similar villages and churches throughout the land. And yet here is somewhere quite special and unique in the Church of England given its link with the Shrine of Our Lady of Walsingham, originally situated in the parish church and subsequently translated to the separate Shrine church where the image now resides.

It could all have been simply a romantic flight of fancy on the part of Fr Patten, but as Fr Davage well illustrates, that would have been to underestimate not only Fr Patten's determination, in spite of his precarious state of health, but his profound commitment to the catholic cause in the Church of England and not least his fervent devotion to Our Lady. And it is that same commitment and profound devotion which is amply evident in each of his seven successors to the present day – a commitment and devotion which have ensured the sustaining and survival of both parish and Shrine in ways unimaginable 100 years ago. How ironic that those ornaments and practices which caused Fr Patten's run-in with episcopal authority should today be met with unequivocal episcopal - even archiepiscopal - approval. But then that would be true of many priests and parishes in the early years of the catholic movement, which led to some priests even being imprisoned.

This account of the *Vicars of Walsingham* gives us a fascinating insight into each of their backgrounds – so varied, their personalities, the challenges they faced in the parish and more widely, the sensitivities needed in their relationships with the Shrine, and its Administrator and Guardians – and Fr Davage in no way evades the stresses and strains which have from time to time been very evident between the two. Similarly, the relationship between the Vicar of Walsingham and the Roman Catholic priest was fraught and frosty in the beginning; but when the former Vicar of Walsingham Fr Rear, in the wake of his predecessor's being received into the Church of Rome, himself became a Roman Catholic, was ordained and returned to Walsingham to the Roman Catholic Shrine, this perceived insensitivity could have made for a considerable set-back in the relationship between the two churches. As it happened, with Fr Haydon's appointment the reverse became true and relations were strengthened and improved enormously and fortunately flourish to the present day. I remember one occasion at a large gathering in Walsingham, Bishop Alan Clark, the first bishop of the newly created Diocese of East Anglia, and himself the son of parents who converted from the Church of England to the Roman Catholic Church, speaking of the two Shrines in the one domain.

Reading through this fascinating account of these eight priests over 100 years I could not but be struck by their unerring faith and faithfulness to their priestly and pastoral calling. No ministry and management here for them, nor the barren and dry land of café church and Messy Church and fluid church, but ever mindful of the 'dignity' and 'great importance' of the priestly office as the Book of Common Prayer Ordinal has it. They pursued unerringly that with which they had been charged – 'to feed and provide for the Lord's family; to seek for Christ's sheep that are dispersed abroad, and for his children who are in the midst of this naughty world; that they may be saved through Christ for ever'. Antiquated language it may be, nevertheless it sums up what has been described as the 'priest-like task' in every age. The current Ordinal puts it more succinctly with regard to the responsibility and relationship of the priest to the people – 'Serve them with joy, build them up in faith'.

At the very heart and centre of their whole lives, that which motivates and encourages, that which enlivens and constantly reinvigorates them is the celebration of that 'full, perfect, and sufficient sacrifice' offered daily in the sacrifice of the Mass. As Michael Ramsey puts it 'at the altar the priest is drawn terribly and wonderfully near not only to the benefits of Christ's redemption but to the redemptive act itself'. And it is from this that all else flows – so clearly evident in the lives of these vicars of Walsingham. In their multifarious ministrations

– sacramental, pastoral, practical – their engagement not only with the church but with the whole village community.

This riveting and informative profile of the eight vicars and parish of Walsingham could be construed as a very practical and down to earth account of the catholic movement in the Church of England over 100 years. The Second Vatican Council was a huge influence in its ecclesiology, the shift in liturgical understanding and practice with the introduction of nave altars following, the 'westward position' for the Eucharistic celebration, evening Masses which would have been taboo in Fr Patten's day and as was certainly my own experience too in my early days – and so much more which in fact came to influence liturgical revision and practice more widely in the Church of England as a whole. All of this is to be found in Fr Davage's book.

More recently of course has been the decision of the Church of England to admit women to the presbyterate and the episcopate – a decision which has brought so much upheaval to so many priests, people and parishes, again well reflected in these pages. What would Fr Patten have made of one of his successors becoming a Provincial Episcopal Visitor? The good news of course is that, as any one of the Episcopal Visitors will tell you, parishes and priests such as Walsingham still flourish despite, in some places, every effort to persuade and influence them otherwise, not least by some of the present episcopate.

In all, what we have here in *Vicars of Walsingham* is a very readable and hugely encouraging account of eight very different people called by God to serve his Church on earth. What has struck me most in reading through this book is the sheer devotion and unfailing commitment and service often at considerable cost to themselves of these 'vicars' and in some cases their families too – after the example of the One who came 'not to be served but to serve and give his life as a ransom for many'. Above all, given as with every human person, their vulnerabilities, their failings, their weaknesses and yes their strengths too it is God's abundant mercy and grace which shine through their endeavours at every stage. It is Hans Urs von Balthasar who writes 'A good priest is always a miracle of grace'. Here thanks be to God are eight exemplars of such a 'miracle of grace'.

✱David M Hope
February 2021

ACKNOWLEDGEMENTS

Fr William Davage
*was Priest Librarian and Custodian
of the Library, Pusey House, Oxford
1994 – 2011*

I am immensely grateful to all those who have assisted in the writing of this book. I am particularly indebted to those former Incumbents who wrote comprehensive accounts of their backgrounds and ministries, spoke to me, answered questions, provided comments and corrections of fact or interpretation, and so much else essential to this undertaking. They bear no responsibility for what I have written, *quod scripsi, scripsi*, but none of it would have been possible without their keen interest and generous contributions.

My gratitude is also owed to current members of the congregation for speaking or writing to me: Betty Howe, Graham Howard, Brian Landale, Monica Smith, Lynette Sutton.

I also benefited, with gratitude, from the assistance and memories of Fr Christopher Colven former Priest Administrator of the Shrine of Our Lady of Walsingham. My thanks are also owed to the hospitality of the present Administrator, Fr Kevin Smith and the, then, Shrine Priest Fr Andreas Wenzel, and the Staff of the Shrine where much of the research and background reading for the book was undertaken in the two weeks before the closure caused by the Covid-19 pandemic.

As many will be aware, no book on Walsingham is possible without the assistance and knowledge of Isabel Syed, the Honorary Archivist of the Shrine. Our contact had to be by email during the disruption of the pandemic and she pointed me to valuable material and, not least, for her participation in a spirited tripartite correspondence about how Fr Patten morphed into Fr Hope Patten.

We were joined in that exchange by Michael Yelton. When Michael learned that I was to write this book he wrote to me offering any assistance he could and allowing me to use any material from his book *Alfred Hope Patten and the Shrine of Our Lady of Walsingham* (Canterbury Press 2006). My chapter on Fr Patten will illustrate my indebtedness and gratitude to his definitive work. It is cited in the Footnotes as Yelton.

As well as being one of the former Incumbents and the subject of a chapter in this book, Fr Michael Rear has written a very fine history *Walsingham: Pilgrims and Pilgrimage* (Gracewing 2019 2nd Edition) and earns my additional thanks. It is cited in the Footnotes as Rear.

Fr Colin Stephenson, who succeeded Fr Patten as Master of the Guardians and Administrator of the Shrine, wrote wittily and a little naughtily about Anglo-Catholicism. His books *Walsingham Way* (Darton, Longman and Todd 1970) and *Merrily on High* remain a joy. The former is cited in the Footnotes as Stephenson.

I am grateful to the Principal and Chapter of Pusey House, Oxford for access to their Library holdings and especially to Fr James Mosher who undertook research during the pandemic restrictions which prevented me from travelling to Oxford.

Several friends, to whom I am grateful, have indulged me during the writing of the book: Fr Robert Coates, who provided material for one of the chapters, Fr Paul Conrad, Fr James Patrick, Fr Nicholas Burton, Fr Barry Orford, Glynn Smith, Denis Moriarty, Matthew Chinery, and Karol Danielewicz. Thanks to Stephen Parkinson for commenting on the first draft of each chapter and for assistance with particular points of detail that arose during each stage of the writing and promptly finding the information that I needed. And two friends in particular: Nathan Paine Davey who was at Walsingham with me in March 2020 for much fun and companionship; Fr Hugh Mead who generously agreed to read and comment on drafts of the chapters as they were written. His scholarly eye saved me from solecisms, redundancies, omissions, and infelicities. I am deeply grateful. Also to Judith Mead for her additional comments. Any errors or inadequacies which remain are entirely mine.

And to Fr Harri Williams for inviting me to write the book; to him and Clare for generous hospitality; and for continuing valued friendship. His is a short chapter but however long or short his Incumbency, I am certain his will be a formidable and outstanding contribution to the life, ministry and worship of this parish and the wider church.

This book has been conceived as a series of profiles of the parish priests since 1921 as part of the commemoration of the centenary of Fr Alfred Hope Patten's Induction as Vicar. It might be helpful to indicate what the book is not. It is not intended to be a history of the parish, although parish life and the contribution of the Incumbents to that life will feature. Nor is it intended, in the case of Fr Patten, to be a history of the Shrine of Our Lady of Walsingham, nor a definitive biography of him, nor one that would impair the balance of the book. His life and work have been generously covered by Michael Yelton. Nor is it intended to be a history of the village of Walsingham for which Fr Michael Rear has written the most comprehensive account.

ALFRED HOPE PATTEN

F r Alfred Hope Patten was inducted as Vicar of Great and Little Walsingham with Houghton on 19th January 1921. He was in office for 37 years until his death on 11th August 1958. As the restorer of the Shrine of Our Lady of Walsingham, desecrated and destroyed at the Reformation, he won his place in the Pantheon of Anglo-Catholicism, among the Immortals, the "giants in the land." That significant and lasting achievement, however, began in, and was rooted in, the parish of which he was Incumbent.

He was born on 17th November 1885 in Sidmouth, Devon. He was rarely forthcoming about his background. He was born in the Town Brewery where his father may have been manager, later he was a wine and spirit merchant. Drink may have curtailed his employment and may explain Fr Patten's abstemiousness. His maternal grandfather was a schoolmaster and owned his own school.[1] Fr Patten, however, strikingly lacked formal secondary education. As his father became unable to work because of an accident, this would have qualified Fr Patten for admission to Christ's Hospital. But he failed the entrance examination in 1896. His mother explained that he was ill when sitting the examination, and he was allowed in later that year. However, he was withdrawn in 1898 as "not strong enough for school life."[2] During his teenage years spent, partly, in Hove and Brighton he was influenced by the several Anglo-Catholic churches built by Fr Arthur Wagner. Beyond Brighton, as an impressionable young man, he met and was influenced by Abbot Aelred Carlyle, a charismatic pioneer of revived monasticism in the Church of England that had been given general approval by the Archbishop of Canterbury. Fr Patten did not have a university education but was trained for the priesthood

---

1   Yelton Ch.1 gives a full account of the limited information available.
2   I am grateful to Clifford Jones, a museum volunteer at the School, for this information.

at Lichfield Theological College. Ordained deacon in 1913 and to the priesthood the following year, and, as was at the time common practice, he served a succession of curacies. Initially at Holy Cross, Cromer Street, near St Pancras and King's Cross, then, from 1915 S. Alban, Teddington. In 1919 he spent a few months at S. Michael, Ladbroke Grove, served as *locum tenens* at S. Michael, Edinburgh and, finally, at the Good Shepherd, Carshalton. He had also spent a short period at another Wagner church, S. Mary the Virgin, Buxted. Here there was a Walsingham Chapel which replicated the measurements of the medieval Holy House at Walsingham, itself modelled on the Holy House at Nazareth. The Walsingham Chapel became the first restored post-Reformation shrine and doubtless fuelled Fr Patten's Marian ambitions. All had been influenced by the Oxford Movement and the Catholic Revival. His peripatetic clerical apprenticeship ended in 1921 with his appointment to Walsingham.

He arrived in a parish that had already been influenced by the Oxford Movement. Not least through its lay patron, the Lee-Warner family, one of whom had been taught by John Henry Newman at Oriel College. Fr George Ratcliffe Woodward had been appointed in 1882. He had been curate at S. Barnabas, Pimlico that had been in the vanguard of catholic ceremonial and liturgical practice among London churches, the scene of protests and anti-ritualist riots in the past. He had been succeeded by Fr Wanburgh and Fr Reeves, both Anglo-Catholics. There was already an established daily Mass and Fr Reeves had installed a statue of Our Lady in the parish church.[3] It was fertile ground for Fr Patten's ministry.

As he was not faced with a blank canvas, Fr Patten was able to make various changes in the liturgical practice of the parish, some modest but others that marked a significant shift in emphasis. He regularly emphasised the need for and recourse to the sacrament of Confession as an indispensable part of the Christian life and its responsibilities. Incense became a regular feature of sacramental celebrations. The

---

3   Rear p. 203.

BCP Communion Rite was reordered by moving the Gloria in excelsis from the end of Mass to the beginning. The Prayer for the Church Militant was said audibly but the combined Prayers of Consecration and Thanksgiving were said silently with interpolations from the Roman Canon. The liturgical rite was recognisably Book of Common Prayer but was accompanied by Roman ceremonial for which he recruited generations of servers, who alone joined in the responses to the Mass. These changes were not, however, universally popular. In his later years he admitted that "he had made a great mistake when he abandoned the audible saying of parts of the Prayer Book in the parish church. He would not go back on what he had done, but he realised that it had isolated the parish from the main flow of the Church of England."[4]

He came to Walsingham, enchanted with his romanticised vision of the Middle Ages, of England as Mary's Dowry, determined to revive the medieval pilgrimage to Our Lady, and, significantly signalled that intention by changing the dedication of the church by adding S. Mary to the original dedication to All Saints. Marian feasts were kept with due solemnity. In 1922 he commissioned a statue of Our Lady modelled

on the image on a 12th century seal of the former Priory found within its ruins. It was installed in a chapel on the north side of the church, displacing the Lee-Warner family pew, without consultation and to their annoyance. A few days thereafter he founded a devotional guild, which later developed into the Society of Our Lady of Walsingham. These were changes and innovations that built upon rather than replaced existing practices. They may have been the fulfilment of Fr Patten's original intentions and the parish church may have

4   See Stephenson p. 229. Also Yelton p. 46.

remained the centre of the cultus and the destination of the revived pilgrimage on a relatively modest and domestic scale had there not been significant obstacles in his path that would seek to thwart even these changes.

Willingness to compromise or to reverse these perceived objectionable innovations was not the attitude of the Young Turk when taking up his first incumbency in 1921. Of the categories and gradations evident in the Catholic Movement, Fr Patten was firmly and quintessentially among the Anglo-Papalists. He subscribed less to the Thirty-Nine Articles of Religion than to the doctrine and moral teaching of the Catholic Church and the Roman Magisterium, to the authority of Church Councils, including that of Trent and the First Vatican Council (which asserted papal Infallibility), and their decrees, of the Pope and his pronouncements, with the exception of Apostolicæ Curæ, which condemned Anglican Orders as "null and utterly void". Roman in all things but that, and the stipend. It was summed up in his reaction to the death of Pope Benedict XV in 1922: "He was the chief Bishop of the Christian Church, though unfortunately, through quarrels and schisms within the fold of Christ there is no external communion between the Sees of Rome and Canterbury [there are those] wide-minded enough to recognise that when part of Christ's Body, the Church, suffers loss, we all suffer."[5]

He subscribed to the Oxford Movement Centenary Manifesto of 1933 which was the most explicit articulation of the Anglo-Papalist position. Anglo-Papalists viewed the Church of England as a schismatic body, forced into schism by Henry VIII and Elizabeth I. The Church of England was a severed limb of the universal Church containing two provinces and the Anglo-Papalist aim was restore communion with the Pope and the rest of the Catholic Church: the reunion of sister churches rather than the submission of an errant and wayward daughter. "The existence of the Church of England as a body de facto from the rest of the Catholic Church is only tolerable when it

---

5   Walsingham and Houghton Parish Magazine 1922.

is regarded as a temporary evil, destined to disappear when God shall be pleased to restore us to our natural place among our brethren."

Like many others, Fr Patten was among those who did not anticipate that such corporate, sacramental reunion would be achieved in one fell swoop but was convinced that, in due time, from the fragmentation of the one, holy, catholic and apostolic Church, and from the desert experience, as he saw it, of the Church of England, there would emerge corporate reunion. Although viewed by some as absurd, by others as fifth-columnists, the contribution of Anglo-Papalists to ecumenical conversations and tentative steps towards reunion ought not to be underestimated nor under-appreciated. Before the desired reunion could be achieved, and however long-delayed, the ecclesiological wilderness of the Church of England had to be endured as a stepping-stone to that end. Anglo-Papalists had to content themselves to a hybrid existence; Catholic but not Roman, Catholic in belief and practice but Anglican in office and the security of tenure that Freehold allowed, stipend and episcopal obedience but only insofar as it was conscientiously possible.

It was encounters with his diocesan bishop, by correspondence and a memorable meeting in the parish church, that triggered the acquisition of land to build a shrine that would be independent of episcopal authority and interference, and to translate the image of Our Lady from the parish church. The Oxford Movement had been predicated on the doctrine of Apostolic Succession, of an episcopal line in the English Church from S. Peter continued uninterrupted, as a golden thread, through the doctrinal turmoil of the Reformation. Respect for the doctrine was often accompanied by misgivings

Translation of the image on 15th October 1931

about the holders of the office. A high regard for episcopacy went alongside a low view of individual bishops. There was often felt a pressing need to hold base individuals to the high dignity of their office. As Colin Stephenson laconically commented, "authority has always been a weak point in the Anglo-Catholic armoury."[6]

It was a mark of the success of Fr Patten's revived devotion to Our Lady, the installation of a new statue, and the encouragement of pilgrimage that it came to the bishop's attention. Their subsequent correspondence was studiously polite but unyielding, as differing, incompatible views were firmly articulated. Nothing of that was altered by the bishop's visit, part of Anglo-Catholic folklore, which saw an insouciant Fr Patten escort an increasingly anxious Dr Pollock around the church, pointing out the Confessional and the statue of Our Lady that seemed to have missed the bishop's attention, possibly deliberately so. The bemused and hapless bishop was heard to mutter that matters were far worse than he had supposed or feared. Whereas Fr Patten had created at Walsingham a model of what he thought the Church of England should look like and be, it was not a vision recognised nor shared by Bishop Pollock.[7] He required the removal of the offending innovations. Subsequent clashes did exhibit the occasional note of asperity, with Fr Patten, not overawed by the social and educational advantages of the bishop that he lacked and, of which, he was sometimes painfully aware, ending one spat with a tart rejoinder that "I refuse to do anything more in the matter."[8]

Given episcopal hostility, it was politic to create, or, as he would have seen it, re-create a place for devotion to Our Lady and a destination for Marian pilgrims outside the parish church. That might have been in Fr Patten's mind for some time as, subsequent to the bishop's visit, he conceded that the image of Our Lady had not been originally in the parish church and that he might contemplate finding some private

---

6   Stephenson pp. 111.
7   Stephenson p. 112.
8   Yelton p. 108.

land where a small chapel could be built to house the statue.[9] The building of the present Shrine is Fr Patten's abiding memorial and his great work. For the rest of his ministry and life, he combined the posts of parish priest and Administrator of the Shrine. While the building of the Shrine and its modest expansion before and after the War took up much of his time and energy, and, inevitably shifted his focus, there may have been required some adjustments to parish routine, he continued to take his responsibilities with due seriousness and attention. The Shrine became part of the life of the parish. Not least in that the limited accommodation for pilgrims in the Shrine at the time meant that many became paying guests of parishioners. Some returned regularly and formed lasting friendships. In its early years and during the War the activity of the Shrine was on a relatively small scale and was not the significant logistical operation that it has become. Village businesses, which were numerous, butchers, grocers, bakeries notable among them, benefited from the custom of pilgrims and other visitors but, ironically, as the Shrine expanded, its season lengthened, particularly in the years after his death, local trades declined and disappeared.

There were undoubtedly some for whom the Shrine was an annoyance and its pilgrims an inconvenience and disruption, and there may have been some that felt that Fr Patten spent too much time on the affairs of the Shrine to the neglect of those of the parish. In his early days in the parish, there were those, some older parishioners, who were devoted to his predecessor and disliked the changes that Fr Patten introduced. That is not unusual in most parishes. Given that Fr Patten arrived with an intention to revive and encourage pilgrimage, he could not have succeeded without substantial goodwill from the congregation and the wider village community. Although naturally shy and reserved he was able, nevertheless, to exert a quiet and compelling authority to which his parishioners became accustomed and attuned. He spoke well, simply, accessibly and persuasively, not

9   Yelton pp 79-81.

least in his sermons which were invariably clear and understandable. His charm and determination attracted many to support his aims.[10]

From the beginning of his ministry he showed an enthusiasm for parish life and was a visible presence in the village; often to be seen cycling around the parish and occasionally in a pony and trap. He showed the characteristic of most Anglo-Catholic priests in being an assiduous, regular and frequent visitor, not only at moments of personal or familial crisis. He showed an interest in and concern for his parishioners and was usually relaxed in their company.[11] The vicarage was something of an open house with boisterous evening suppers a particular feature.[12] He was regarded as rather more approachable than some of his more remote predecessors.

As a large part of his time saw him engaged on Shrine business, he was fortunate to be supported for many years by Fr Derrick Lingwood. He was a local boy whose potential and abilities had been recognised by Fr Patten who encouraged him in a priestly vocation. He was also crucially involved with the work of the Shrine from its inception. As the highly efficient and competent Bursar, he provided the practical and financial acumen, a solid base for Fr Patten's more mercurial ideas and imaginative fantasies. Fr Patten's own finances were invariably chaotic. Fr Colin Stephenson maintained that, as Fr Patten became increasingly: "more engaged by his vision, or successive visions, for the Shrine and the extension of its life," Fr Lingwood, "in large measure, if not entirely, ran the parishes and provided pastoral care."[13] As well as the Shrine, it seems clear that Fr Patten's focus was more on S. Mary's and that Fr Lingwood was particularly active at S. Peter's. One parishioner commented that Fr Patten stopped coming. But Fr Lingwood did not have an entirely free hand. He thought that the more pastorally appropriate and sensitive liturgical provision at

---

10   Stephenson pp 106-108.
11   Yelton p. 46.
12   Stephenson p. 108.
13   Stephenson p. 222.

S. Peter's ought to be BCP but this was vetoed by Fr Patten. When Betty Howe, a parishioner at S. Mary's who knew every Incumbent from Fr Patten to the present day, was asked whether it was true that Fr Lingwood did most of the pastoral work in the parish, she replied, decisively, "Oh no. Fr Patten was in charge."[14] Fr Lingwood's pastoral work in S. Peter's and in the new housing estate in Great Walsingham may have given rise to the presumption that Fr Patten's work in the Shrine and at S. Mary's was at the expense of the new estate and S. Peter's in which he evinced limited interest.

The extent of Fr Patten's practical and emotional reliance on Fr Lingwood was thrown into sharp relief in the mid 1950s. Fr Stephenson observed that as Fr Patten grew older he became "in some ways more difficult and impossible" as the rift between him and Fr Lingwood painfully illustrated. Once he had decided on a course of action, he became stubbornly immoveable and deaf to advice or notes of caution from others. According to Fr Stephenson the rift seems to have begun as Fr Patten, always on the Anglo-Papalist spectrum of Anglo-Catholicism moved further in that direction, probably influenced by Fr Henry Fynes-Clinton, one of the earliest supporters of the Shrine, Rector of S. Magnus the Martyr, London Bridge, Priest Director of the Sodality of the Precious Blood, Guardian of the Shrine and friend of Fr Patten. Fr Lingwood, as seen by his liturgical preference for S. Peter's, was much less papalistic and much more committed, as Fr Patten had taught him, to the Catholic Faith of the English Church. That may seem something of a wafer-thin disagreement and, without Fr Patten's prickly carapace and sublimated emotions may not have amounted to much. However, Fr Lingwood "committed" matrimony which came as an immense blow to Fr Patten. So close had been their working and personal relationship that Fr Patten felt wounded and rejected, "felt abandoned," according to Fr Stephenson.[15] Fr Lingwood left Walsingham to be the Incumbent of S. Martin, Barton in the

---

14   In conversation March 2020.
15   Stephenson p. 225.

diocese of Exeter. The distance from Walsingham mirroring the fissure in their relationship.[16]

Fr Lingwood's absence, defection as Fr Patten saw it, meant that Fr Patten was "forced once again to take up the reins as parish priest" in Fr Stephenson's words. Even if that is too dramatic a characterisation, it is demonstrable that Fr Lingwood's departure meant that there was more pastoral work for Fr Patten to do and less sharing in liturgical duties. He proved resilient enough and was able to maintain a heavy commitment and "to keep things going without relaxing any traditions." It was the continuation of these traditions to which his mind was turning as he aged. Without Fr Lingwood at his side the future seemed suddenly uncertain. This was exacerbated by a deterioration of his health and failing eyesight. Despite support and assistance from several friends and devotees, notably John Shepherd and Stanley Smith, the latter who served as Churchwarden and Treasurer as well as Bursar of the Shrine, he was concerned about both the future of the parish and anxious about the governance of the Shrine after his death. That death came relatively swiftly and suddenly, even fittingly, on 11th August 1958 when he suffered a heart attack moments after officiating at Benediction of the Blessed Sacrament.

Fr Patten's place in the history of the Catholic Revival is assured. His achievements remain obvious and a lasting tribute to his faith and tenacity. Yet his personality remains tantalisingly out of reach, sometimes contradictory, complicated, and elusive.

A critic once wrote about the novelist and poet Thomas Hardy as "an almost comically neurotic man, from boyhood one who could not bear to be alone; a successful self-made man who was nonetheless given to anxiety and black depression, and whose words increasingly expressed a radical pessimism, a conviction that some dark force controls us since childhood … No-one … could quite understand where his pessimism came from, since his childhood was serene,

---

16   There was a subsequent easing of the rift and a degree of rapprochement that Fr Lingwood sang Fr Patten's Requiem Mass.

his adult life a series of triumphs and his old age covered in glory."[17] Although not entirely congruent, they could be applied, *mutatis mutandis* to Fr Patten, his character and personality.

The most abiding image of Fr Patten is a glacial mask, a severe public façade looking out uneasily from many formal photographs. But there is one set of photographs where he is positively jaunty; posing wearing a hat at several angles and, seemingly, enjoying the experience.[18] These contrasting images are two aspects of his character and are not, necessarily, contradictory. He was austere, disciplined, single-minded, driven, obstinate even. Fr Stephenson maintained that "he found buildings far more easy to manage than human beings."[19] He was a bad chairman and not a committee man. He was stern and could be ruthless when crossed. Yet he attracted many to share his vision and implement his ambition. He had the ability to inspire, to communicate his enthusiasm to them and persuade them to join him in a major endeavour. He was immensely, robustly engaging and resourceful, harnessing the commitment and energies of others, with abilities and expertise which he lacked.

Once the Shrine was established, he expended much time and energy in a series of attempts to establish a communal, or quasi-monastic community, echoing the early influence of Aelred Carlyle, but he was drawn to solitude. Although his vicarage was accessible to all, he needed to withdraw from the pressure of parish and communal life from time to time. Michael Yelton makes the point that, although he was at ease visiting his parishioners, he was only fully relaxed in the company of those whom he did not regard as intellectual rivals.[20] Although obviously intelligent, he was not an intellectual. He was

---

17   Carole Angier, *Literary Review* 2006.
18   Michael Yelton, Alfred Hope Patten: His Life and Times in Pictures. Anglo-Catholic History Society [2007]. No longer available from the ACHS but, according to the Society's website, a 2013 reprint is available from The Shrine Shop in Walsingham.
19   Stephenson p. 235.
20   Yelton p. 46.

strikingly lacking in formal education, something he felt keenly. He spent short periods at Christ's Hospital and Reigate Grammar School, and some time at a boarding school in Eastbourne.[21] He had not been to university and often exhibited a prickly defensiveness and an auto-didacticism, often the resort of those who feel on shaky social or intellectual ground, that did not respond well to criticism nor opposition. He had, for example, a decided reluctance to employ Latin in the liturgy, which was one symptom among several aspects of his life where he showed a marked inferiority complex, both academically and socially.

He was conscious of his social background and social standing in the community. He did not fit the social profile of traditional Norfolk incumbents who were scions of local aristocratic families or the gentry, or fitted well into that milieu. He was not subsumed into the squirearchy.[22] Although his relations with local clergy were polite, he played little part in rural deanery affairs[23] and his celibate status may have contributed to him being seen as aloof.

To compensate for his social unease and sense of inferiority, he would not be alone in having delusions of grandeur. As the Oxford Movement looked back to a pre-Reformation ideal of a united, undivided western Church, the aesthetic impulse of the Movement was, similarly, a consciously revivified medievalism. This was most obviously evident in the Gothic Revival in architecture, not least church buildings, and the subject matter of many paintings of the Pre-Raphaelite Brotherhood, and, influenced by medieval guilds and artisan skills, the artefacts, decorative schemes and buildings of the Arts and Crafts Movement. Fr Patten combined those instincts, that romanticised medievalism, with a love of the baroque. In his restoration of the Shrine and its governance, he solicited the support of many with aristocratic connections and titles, recognising the cachet

---

21 Yelton Ch. 1.
22 Yelton p. 45.
23 Stephenson p. 120.

and the cash that they might bring. He kitted out the Guardians, and himself as Master with an impressive chain of office, as bargain-basement Knights of the Garter. Their stalls in the choir of the Shrine

Church display their coats of arms. He had a keen interest in heraldry. At a Requiem Mass on the death of Queen Alexandra he erected a large catafalque that was adorned with several relevant heraldic and armorial devices, surmounted by black ostrich feathers. He instituted something like an Honours system in the Clerks and Dames of the Holy House: more MBE than KBE.

He greatly disliked his first Christian name, Alfred, rarely, if ever, using it. In correspondence he invariably signed letters 'A Hope Patten'. Hope is his second Christian name but it is also a common surname. Without any deliberation on his part, it may have been assumed to be a surname and he may have been happily aware of its quasi-aristocratic resonance not to disabuse any assumptions others might mistakenly make. It would not be inconsistent with other aspects of his personality. It would, either consciously or unconsciously, compensate for his relatively modest background. It would also chime with his childhood imagination and even, perhaps a hint of wishful thinking.[24]

---

24 In an email discussion Isabel Syed, Michael Yelton and I were agreed that he disliked the name Alfred but disagreed on whether or not the use of Hope had some element of deliberation as a surname. His friends called him Hope and Michael Yelton remarked that some also called him Pat. I was more sceptical, given the propensity of some priests, of a certain generation and disposition to call one another Father, even in private conversation

Highly-strung, neurotic, prone to nervous debility and exhaustion, alleviated by periods of absence, sometimes travelling in Europe driven by Stanley Smith. He may not have had the "radical pessimism" attributed to Thomas Hardy but he had a depressive streak and a darker side to his character. He took an interest in the occult and was not unwilling to attribute ghostly, other-worldly activity to mundane events. This interest in the paranormal and psychic communications bears the imprint of Abbot Carlyle. Strengths can also be, as Michael Yelton observes, "to some extent a defect or weakness in character." He may have possessed a powerful but narrow focus, a single-mindedness of purpose but that had the effect of isolating and not concerning himself "with many of the preoccupations of the general population." He was not interested in current affairs, sport, food or wine.[25] He was rigidly orthodox, demanded of himself the highest standards of propriety, had a strict code of behaviour and expected the highest standards in others. Intolerance, impatience, implacable obstinacy were not unknown. These and similar traits became increasingly set in stone as he grew older. And so the epithets multiply and build up: *pelion on ossa.*

They cannot be dismissed as eccentricities or quirks but they are important elements, aspects of a complicated individual and personality that must be seen in a wider context. They cannot and do not define the whole man. He was conscious of his office and the demands made on him and the expectations of parishioners. He had an imposing presence, "tall, handsome and … great dignity of

---

and I had great difficulty in imagining anyone calling him Pat to his face and wondered if that was what friends called him when talking between themselves about him. Certainly in more recent years common usage has morphed from Fr Patten to Fr Hope Patten. I was guilty of it in a sermon on the 50th anniversary of his death. Those parishioners, like Betty Howe, who knew him always refer to him as Fr Patten, as does Isabel Syed, and, now, me.

25   Yelton p. 42.

bearing."[26] He was self-disciplined and expected discipline in others. Pilgrims and parishioners saw in him a figure of dignity, charm and innate spirituality. He may have become more remote in his later years, to which his deteriorating eyesight may have contributed and gave rise to that perception.

A letter from five years into his incumbency gives a different insight into his character and of his pastoral engagement in the parish. Canon John Blake-Humphrey, in a letter to Samuel Gurney[27], the high-church brother of Fr Patten's low-church patron, Sir Eustace Gurney[28], wrote that Fr Patten exhibited "a loving, sympathetic manner," provided a "listening ear," that he was "approachable [and] winsome," he created a "spiritual atmosphere ... of the very highest order," and that "congregations at all services are always large and have vastly increased and are increasing."[29] Although it was an age of deference, that is not sufficient enough reason to elicit such an appreciation. Respect, affection and love for him are still expressed by those who knew and remembered him as their parish priest. Fr Keith Haydon recalls that as a child he visited Walsingham and in the Pilgrims' Hall heard "gales of laughter" from Fr Patten's table.[30] Several of his angularities clearly softened and much of his reserve dissipated when faced with practical, pastoral concerns, particularly encountering people at moments of acute vulnerability and pain.

The most detailed memories of Fr Patten's pastoral ministry were written by Dick Crowe in 2008 when he was aged 81.[31] In 1939 Fr Bernard Walke, the parish priest of S. Hilary, Cornwall, evacuated 11 children from the orphanage to Walsingham. Dick Crowe was one of

---

26   Isabel Syed in correspondence
27   He paid for the work of Martin Travers in the church of S. Swithun, Compton Beauchamp. He lived in the Old Rectory.
28   The Lee-Warner family had failed in the male line and the patronage passed by marriage into the low-church, banking family of the Gurneys.
29   Rear p. 204.
30   In conversation.
31   Walsingham Anglican Archives.

them. Fr Walke and his church had been subject to much protestant harassment, disruption and vandalism in opposition to his ritual innovations of liturgy and devotional images. The orphanage run by the church was collateral damage. The children were originally intended to be housed in Knight Street but the two cottages were not available for some time. As a temporary measure they lodged with parishioners. After some time, with Knight Street still unavailable, Fr Walke's pocket could not meet the additional expense. Within a relatively short time, the children moved into the vicarage and remained there until 1945 when the boys and girls moved into The Falcons in Wells Road. As the boys and girls became adults, they moved away. Rather, than retain a mixed house, it gradually became an all boys Home until its closure.

Significantly, the original children often returned to visit bringing with them boyfriends, girlfriends, wives, husbands and their children. Dick Crowe remembered that Fr Patten had "played a hugely significant part in my life and made me what I am today." He also remembered Fr Lingwood as a "kind man, who was always under great stress trying to raise money to pay for the running costs of the Shrine and the S. Hilary's Children's Home" (formerly The Falcons). Another example of the symbiotic relationship between Frs Patten and Lingwood. On the children's arrival in 1939, duly apprehensive, they were welcomed by Fr Patten. "I remember a kindly man who put us at our ease." Dick Crowe had not liked the Home in Cornwall but "from the moment I met Fr Patten my fears were dispelled. He was so easy to get on with and so approachable. I took to him straight away and, as it turned out, he became the most caring person I had known since I had left London six years earlier."

On life in the vicarage, Dick Crowe wrote with equal warmth. He appreciated that it was something of a major change, even intrusion, into Fr Patten's life to have 10 children in residence and at a time when he had spent so much physical, mental and nervous energy on the building and development of the Shrine, and the increased emotional stress on the outbreak of war. It would have been understandable and excusable had he not taken them in at all, or, having done so, guarded his privacy, insisted on a rigid regime. Yet Dick Crowe's memoir shows that was far from the day to day reality of life in the vicarage. "I really do think he enjoyed it," he wrote. As Dick Crowe remembered, "I had never been so happy as I was at that period of my life." Far from remote or forbidding, Fr Patten "was always available if we needed to talk." Fr Patten would allow Dick into his study even when writing a sermon and accepted Dick's childish offer to help him. Fr Patten taught him to play chess. When he wished to finish the sermon, he sent Dick out with a mock stern voice.

Dick's first experience of a holiday was with Fr Patten at Grasmere in the Lake District. They saw Wordsworth's Cottage, walked in the hills, beside lakes and waterfalls. Fr Patten "loved to walk and would tell me about his future plans for the Shrine and College." In retrospect Dick thought that it was Fr Patten's "escapism from detractors and financial worries." There was something child-like in Fr Patten's nature, a degree of innocence, naïveté perhaps, even the tantrums and

obstinacy, that made him at ease in the company of children. Only then did he feel able to relax his guard and lower his defensive shield and emerge from his protective emotional shell. Dick Crowe's conclusion was that his time living in Walsingham with Fr Patten "changed my life and in my view the miracle of Our Lady of Walsingham is Fr Hope Patten because without him none of it would have happened." In his 81st year Dick Crowe laid flowers on Fr Patten's grave in remembrance and thanksgiving.

ALAN ARTHUR ROE

Fr Alan Arthur Roe was inducted to the Living in Spring 1959.[32] He was a "Norfolk man."[33] At the end of his first year at Walsingham, he wrote that he felt, "you have let me off the usual fifteen years probation before a stranger is accepted as part of a village."[34] He trained for the priesthood at Kelham Theological College, near Newark. Staffed by members of the Society of the Sacred Mission, it provided training for non-graduate ordinands and produced many faithful priests in the Catholic tradition. Fr Roe was ordained deacon in 1951 and to the priesthood in 1952. He served curacies in two distinguished Anglo-Catholic parishes; S. Giles, Reading (1951-1955) and S. John the Evangelist, Newbury (1955-1959). In his final year in Newbury (1958-1959) he was Curate in Charge of S. George's Conventional District. Walsingham was his first, and only, incumbency. He retired, owing to ill-health, in 1977 having served for 18 years, second in length only to Fr Patten.

Walsingham had become, under Fr Patten, a significant Anglo-Catholic parish renowned beyond its boundaries. Fr Roe faced a daunting task. He had to follow a long, nationally recognised incumbent, one who had become a hero of the Anglo-Catholic Movement. It would have been challenging enough simply to have followed Fr Patten but he also had as the new Administrator of the Shrine, Fr Colin Stephenson. He had succeeded Fr Patten as Master of the Guardians and as Administrator. To complicate matters, during the Interregnum it had been suggested, and by some anticipated, that Fr Stephenson should combine the roles of parish priest and Administrator, a continuation of Fr Patten's ministry. That did not

---

32   The exact date could not be found in the records that survived the fire of 1961, when the Service Registers were destroyed.

33   Rear p. 225.

34   Parish Magazine May 1960.

appeal to Fr Stephenson then but later he came to regret it.[35] In retrospect he thought that he could have combined the two. The pilgrimage season in those days was busy but short. Much shorter and less busy, a much smaller operation than it is today. The rest of the year was fallow. "Following Fr Patten must have been hard enough, but to have the extrovert Colin next door was exceedingly difficult."[36]

Compared with the ebullient, witty, imposing Fr Stephenson, Fr Roe was a "quiet, family man, homely, approachable."[37] However different in temperament and character, Fr Roe had to disentangle the parish from the Shrine and restore a distinctly independent parish ministry. It was impossible to ignore the Shrine and its work, or to underestimate the fact that pilgrims to the Shrine contributed to the parish. A new relationship had to be established recognising their different and complementary roles. Differences in temperament and character between Fr Roe and Fr Stephenson also contributed to both parish and Shrine following independent paths.

Fr Roe's appointment as parish priest inevitably meant a break with the past and a different way from that of Fr Patten. Not least that Fr Roe was married to Heather and had a daughter Veronica. But the change can also be seen in a wider context. Only 59 days after Fr Patten's death, Pope Pius XII died; and 19 days later the election and subsequent coronation of Pope John XXIII to a pontificate which was to have far-reaching effects in the Catholic Church, and beyond. Without forcing the comparison too greatly, nor make it too fanciful: whereas Fr Patten represented the passing age, Fr Roe was the harbinger of change. As the spare austerity of Pope Pius gave way to the robust geniality of Pope John, so the austere Fr Patten gave way to the approachable Fr Roe.

Fr Roe had a great admiration for Pope John. He appreciated the Pope's openness, his calling of the Ecumenical Council (Vatican II)

---

35   Rear p. 224.
36   Fr Rear in correspondence.
37   Betty Howe in conversation.

in 1962 and enthusiastically supported the changes it brought about, ecumenically and liturgically, under Pope John's successor, Pope Paul VI. Before the Council was convened, Fr Roe was encouraged by the visit of the Archbishop of Canterbury, Geoffrey Fisher, to Pope John. Fr Roe was an ecumenist and shared the Anglo-Catholic desire for Christian Unity, tempered by an appreciation of the difficulties that needed to be overcome. Reconciliation rather than submission was the Anglo-papalist goal. He wrote, "No Christian ... can approve of such division ... Some members of the Church desire reunion so much that they are apt to overlook the differences that separate us. True union cannot ... be brought about by closing our eyes to the real differences in belief and organisation which unhappily exist."[38]

While recognising the stumbling blocks, he had warm personal relationships with the Roman Catholic parish priest. When Fr Gerard Hulme moved from Walsingham to Sheringham in 1968, Fr Roe wrote that they had always enjoyed a close and warm relationship and described him as a "pioneer in fostering good relations." In receiving a cheque from Fr Roe, Fr Hulme commented that, "it must be historic to have your congregation make a farewell collection for a Roman Catholic priest," which he accepted as "a gesture of kindness and fellowship."[39]

The previous year Fr Roe and Fr Stephenson had attended a meeting held in Walsingham to discuss ecumenical co-operation which had resulted in the formation of the Ecumenical Society of the Blessed Virgin Mary. Fr Stephenson said that Anglicans desired to share whatever they had with their Roman brethren and Fr Roe said that, subject to episcopal approval, S. Mary's would be available and would support the activities of the Society. Towards the end of Fr Roe's incumbency ecumenical relations had warmed to such an extent that in 1975, the The Rt Revd Alan Clark, then Titular Bishop of Elmham and Auxiliary Bishop in the diocese of Northampton, and

---

38   Parish Magazine January 1961.
39   Parish Magazine March 1968.

more significantly, Joint Chairman of the Anglican-Roman Catholic International Commission (ARCIC),[40] preached at the service for Christian Unity in January and at the Feast of the Assumption in August.

Liturgical reform and revision of the Missal came in the wake of the Council and effected significant change in parish liturgies, most notably the Mass said no longer in Latin but in the vernacular. The influence of these changes was seen in the Walsingham churches. North Norfolk became an unusual microcosm of the diverse reaction to the liturgical reforms. Fr Roe, an Anglican in the Catholic tradition, warmly embraced and implemented the changes, whereas a few miles away in Downham Market, the Roman Catholic parish priest, Fr Oswald Baker, fought a spirited rear-guard action in his refusal to implement the new liturgical norms and continued to celebrate Mass in Latin in the Tridentine Rite.

As early as 1960, in his first year, Fr Roe showed an awareness that liturgical reform was in the air. He pointed out that in the Roman Catholic Church on the continent, there had been many changes which emphasised "the corporate nature of the Body of Christ." It was rare to find a church where Mass was celebrated without congregations saying their private prayers. The Mass was a corporate action, the work of a community not a collection of individuals. In the months immediately after his arrival he indicated that he did not intend to make sweeping changes but said, in his first sermon, that the church had to move with the times. He was concerned that few people in the congregation were joining in audibly and he urged everyone to join in the congregational responses and other parts and to contribute to a greater sense of corporate worship. It took a little

---

40   The Rt Revd Alan Clark (1919-2002) was appointed first Bishop of East Anglia in 1976 and served until his retirement in 1995. He died in 2002 and is buried in the National Shrine of Our Lady of Walsingham.

time for improvement. He reported that his appeal had achieved "a good start" but that it was still "half-hearted and uncertain."[41]

The Vatican Council ended in 1965. In that year the Church of England Assembly passed a Measure that began a period of liturgical revision overseen by the Liturgical Commission. There followed a series of books marking progressive stages of revision. Series 1 was in large measure the 1928 Prayer Book which had failed to gain Parliamentary approval but had been in use with the Archbishops' *imprimatur.* Series 2 saw a book influenced by the liturgical scholar Dom Gregory Dix OSB, a monk of Nashdom Abbey, which followed the pattern of the Communion Rite which he advocated. Its essential elements being offertory, consecration, fraction, communion. S. Mary's used the Communion Rite in Series 2 on an experimental basis. Fr Roe expressed his approval that the language was "brief and to the point." He told his people that the changes in the text did not change doctrines nor belief of the Church. The new words did "the same things as before." The congregational responsibilities had increased in that there was more participation with the celebrant: the congregation was a more active participant than a passive observer. The Asperges were no longer part of the Introductory Rite, the Kyries were sung in English, the Gloria would be sung by all if the Mass setting permitted. The most obvious physical change was a nave altar with the celebrant facing the people.[42] Fr Roe later reported that many visitors had said how impressed they had been by the passing of the Kiss of Peace to every member of the congregation.[43] One visitor to the parish wrote: "I found the Parish Mass an uplifting experience. It was well filled on a day that was not special, the singing was splendid and the cries of infants made me feel at home." Series 2 was used with the priest facing the people and the congregation sat for the hymns. At the Kiss of Peace, "Duty sidesmen came down the centre shaking

---

41   Parish Magazine April 1960.
42   Parish Magazine 1968. The experiment began on Trinity Sunday.
43   Parish Magazine 1968.

hands with the person at the end of the pew which was passed person to person along the pew."[44]

Series 3 was something of a liturgical *smörgåsbord* with Rites some of which would be acceptable to catholics and others to evangelicals. The final fruit of the series and these experimental liturgies was the Alternative Service Book (ASB). It was a *vade mecum* of Rites and rubrics which permitted a degree of latitude for individual parishes from Roman practice to unadorned evangelical from which conflicting traditions could choose. It introduced a high degree of choice and flexibility, in particular its frequent employment of the phrase "in these or other words." There were two Eucharistic Rites, A and B in traditional and modern language, and four Eucharistic Prayers. There was no longer much that was common in the prayer of the Church of England.

S. Mary's had used some of the experimental liturgy as it appeared, always biased towards Roman practice. The period of experimentation came to an end in 1966. At the Dedication Festival Fr Roe preached a sermon where he contrasted traditional practice and the ethos of the new Rites. The older Rites, he maintained, had been too individualistic. There had been a preponderance of private prayer and devotion with insufficient regard for the corporate nature. Devotions with little or no participation in the Mass setting made the service little more than a concert.

The revision sought to restore an active participation of the people of God in the liturgy of the Church. The emphasis had moved away "from the laws of rubric and outward show towards a real pastoral concern for the spiritual welfare and worship of the Body of Christ." Times of Mass were also changed to reflect a changing pattern of attendance and to introduce an element of flexibility, adapting to the conditions of the day. He reminded his congregation that "it was not holier to attend in the morning rather than an evening Mass." Evening Masses on mid-week days of obligation had been introduced.

---

44   Church Times quoted in Parish Magazine July 1995.

There was also a reduction in gestures for priests and people. "Some unnecessary genuflexion, and signs of the cross have gone" and "fussy birettas are now things of the past." Such liturgical puritanism was a shock to some but embraced by others, not least by Fr Roe.

In a sermon in 1967, he took a wider perspective and pointed out how the liturgical changes that had been introduced were to be seen within that expanded context, that "the whole Christian Church has been in a state of ferment for the past thirty years or so." He maintained that theologians of all denominations had been led by the Holy Spirit towards a greater unity of thought and beyond mere theological speculation. "We are now experiencing the changes in religious thought in our parishes. Our way of worship has been affected, customs of the past hundred years have suddenly changed … almost overnight. Different emphasis is now put upon Christian teachings … A new reformation is certainly taking place in this generation … taking place rapidly … Pope John called it a renewal, a bringing up to date; these and similar changes produced a sense of uncertainty, of anxiety, of disorientation." Of course, the parish priest was at the forefront of many changes but Fr Roe pointed out that these changes were not at the whim of the parish priest, they were the inevitable outcome of a worldwide movement, that the Church was undergoing as a living organism. "If the Church has to follow Christ and manifest Him in the world to any particular generation, it has to learn to adapt … to the needs of that generation and to use as far as possible language and symbols which have meaning to the people of the present time."[45]

On the Feast of the Immaculate Conception in 1968, the Bishop of Lynn consecrated the new nave altar which Fr Roe described as "a revolutionary step for S. Mary's." It had been done "following the practice of the Early Church celebrating Mass over the altar, facing the people," where the Celebrant was "God's agent and the people's representative" acting as "host and President." Echoing the liturgical

---

45   Parish Magazine August 1968.

ethos of his time, he said that "the idea of God being someone far away out towards the East is a concept we must abandon." This polemical trope avoided acknowledging the transcendent God as well as his imminence. Christ had said, "I am in the midst of them"[46] and Fr Roe could not imagine "Jesus turning his back on his friends as priests have done at the altar since medieval times." Fr Roe was relieved that "this practice is fast disappearing in Roman and Church of England services."[47] In 1975 Fr Roe suggested and Fr Alan Carefull, the Administrator of the Shrine agreed that a Pilgrims' Mass at S. Mary's would be the focal point of the weekend pilgrimage. It would be concelebrated and priests from the Shrine would preach regularly. This would also promote unity between the Shrine and the parish. Relations with Fr Carefull were better than those with Fr Stephenson. Fr Roe's successor, Fr John Barnes, gained the impression that Fr Roe felt "demeaned, unappreciated, and persecuted."[48] In these changes Fr Roe was a child of his time.[49] The liturgical changes implemented were but one part of renewal in the parish that came about in the wake of disaster.

Only two years into his incumbency Fr Roe had to face as great a disaster as any parish priest fears and has to endure. On 14th July 1961 the church was set alight.[50] Whether by accident or arson was unclear. On the same night as the fire Dereham Parish Church had been vandalised. It may have been an electrical fault in the organ.[51]

---

46 S. Matthew 18: 20.
47 Parish Magazine December 1968.
48 Fr John Barnes in correspondence.
49 A personal note: There is now neo-Tridentine backlash, or revival is a current liturgical trend. My friend Bishop Jonathan Baker delights to recall that when I was Sacristan at S. Stephen's House, Oxford, he, as a callow first year ordinand, asked me about High Mass. I replied, "High Mass is abolished." He then happily points out that I spent most of my clerical career celebrating High Mass Eastward-facing.
50 The indispensable source is Graham Howard's publication entitled 'A Fire in Walsingham'.
51 Rear p. 225

Whatever the cause, it seems to have begun in the Vestry, Choir Vestry or the Lady Chapel and the damage was extensive.

The alarm was raised by Mrs Gurney from Walsingham Abbey. The fire quickly took hold, with flames shooting through the roof. Windows shattered in the heat, metalwork was twisted and contorted. Despite the best efforts of the fire service, which was quickly on the scene, the roof crashed into the nave. One of the earliest on the scene, Len Whitmore, the Shrine Beadle, realised that nothing could be done. He looked on helpless, with many other parishioners, as word spread and the sounds of sirens and burning were heard in the village.

Other villagers shared similar sentiments as they watched the fire rage and the church reduced to ruins. Fr Stephenson recorded that when he came to the scene he sensed a "feeling of crisis and the whole village was awake, and some were in tears." He saw and heard the roof fall in, "I felt dead and empty" at the scene of such horror.[52] Betty Howe, then village Postmistress, remembered feeling helpless as she stood and stared at the conflagration. Others expressed similar sentiments in the collective grief and horror. Many had gathered and watched anxiously as the steeple threatened to crash and at 11pm heard the clock strike the hour amid the inferno. One who had served

52   Walsingham Review No 2 September 1961.

earlier in the evening at the last service of Benediction thought it seemed like the tolling of a funeral bell. The bells survived the fire. By 11.30pm the fire had been brought under control. Miraculously, the memorial chapel to Fr Patten above the South Porch survived unscathed. The Seven Sacrament Font, among the best in East Anglia, lost its cover and had the stonework marked but survived.

There was some discussion whether or not the church should be rebuilt and repaired or left as a romantic ruin and a new building erected. The decision to rebuild reflected the standing in the village Fr Roe had achieved. He had become a "real village person" and appreciated the iconic status of the church and the affection for it from the villagers. Fr Roe had been away when the fire broke out but received a message that his "church had been razed to the ground." He shared with his Churchwardens and PCC members a determination to rebuild and refused to compromise on its quality and not to make do with second best. They appointed Laurence King to supervise the task. In the meantime services were transferred to S. Peter's.

In May 1962, in wind and rain, Fr Roe celebrated Mass in the ruins to mark the beginning of the restoration work. It was covered by TV and the press. Rebuilding began on 16th May. By August the floors had been levelled, the north  aisle roof and the Lady Chapel had been secured, pillars in the north aisle had been renewed. The south arcade, however, proved too insecure and had to be demolished.[53] Early in the following year, sufficient progress had been made for Fr Roe to conquer his fear of heights and go up to the restored roof space.

Work of this scale and magnitude would once have taken several years, perhaps even a decade. However, it was accomplished within three years and it was thought that it could have been done even more quickly but for a dearth of skilled stonemasons. Fr Roe, with support from his Churchwardens and others, bore a heavy responsibility in discussions with the architect, the builders and the work force, and day to day engagement with any problems that arose, the vagaries of weather among them. In May 1963 he was able to describe the new roof of "gleaming copper" and reported that "inside the ceiling of the nave and chancel are finished and are aglow with beautiful colours as they were in medieval times." He quoted one critic who said that the colours were "too bright" but commented, 'why should our places of worship be draft and mournful?"[54] The church was able to be used from Christmas that year when Midnight Mass was celebrated.

Final touches continued in 1964. The east window was installed in June by John Hayward. It depicted scenes of Lady Richeldis' vision of the Holy House, the House itself, pilgrims to the Shrine, the destruction wrought at the Reformation, the restoration of 1931, the fire and the restored church held in Our Lady's hands. The new organ was inaugurated with a recital by Francis Jackson of York Minster. Relics of S. Thomas of Canterbury, S. Edmund King and Martyr, and S. Edward King and Martyr were enshrined in the altar and the church was consecrated on 8th August 1964. A remarkable achievement but

Fr Roe hands the petition to consecrate the restored S. Mary's to The Rt Revd Launcelot Fleming the Lord Bishop of Norwich

53   Parish Magazine August 1962.
54   Parish Magazine May 1963.

not without financial, psychological and emotional cost. £48,625 was received from the church's insurers and a general appeal raised a further £4.500. Fr Norman Banks wrote that "Walsingham was blessed in having a priest and pastor whose evident faith and love of the Gospel so inspired others that the church was rebuilt in little over three years."[55] Not only did Fr Roe have the rebuilding of S. Mary's to deal with but major work was necessary at S. Peter's where the tower threatened to collapse and repairs required over £7,000 expenditure.

Whereas Fr Roe was on the side of the liberalisation and modernisation of liturgy, he was more staunchly orthodox in his response to the theological ferment that swept through the 1960s and 1970s. One of the first defining, iconoclastic moments which animated public consciousness was the publication of *Honest to God* written by John Robinson, Bishop of Woolwich. Fr Roe had a rather down-to-earth response to the Bishop's argument. Some of the adverse criticism, he maintained, had been caused by the difficulty and confusion of the Bishop's prose. Subsequent to the publication and press and public reaction, the Bishop had needed "to deny many things which he implied in his book. He even accuses the Archbishop of Canterbury for misunderstanding him; if our own very able and learned archbishop [Michael Ramsey] cannot understand the book and does not grasp the thoughts of the Bishop of Woolwich, no wonder that ordinary people like you and me are confused." In retrospect, the book was probably more important for what it represented, or appeared to represent, than for what it, confusedly, said.

In his brief but eloquent riposte, Fr Roe outlined the human limitations of perceiving or talking about the divine, how the concrete nature of human reasoning and perception comes up against the ineffable and transcendent. "We cannot picture God as He is because we cannot see Him and nothing we have seen will do for a likeness … When we need a picture, we should think of Our Lord Jesus Christ, who is both Man and God; who became Man in order that

---

55   In the Foreword to Graham Howard's book.

he could reveal God to mankind." He said that it was beyond our comprehension to picture God's majesty and glory.[56]

Fr Roe also had to deal with the running sore of Anglican-Methodist Reunion which occupied a great deal of time, nervous energy and political manoeuvring until the eventual defeat of the proposals in General Synod. His comments illustrate a thoughtful, measured theological and ecumenical intelligence. As someone committed to ecumenism, he recognised that any reunion would require changes in the traditions of both churches but, as with his ecumenical attitude to Rome, he questioned whether reunion with Methodists should be at any price. He was wary of reunion, at this stage, but rather than erect barriers, he formulated a series of questions which required satisfactory answers or assurances before he could commit to any scheme. Was the Church of England being asked to abandon essential principles and doctrines? Is resistance to reunion a form of conservatism or prejudice? He saw the potential for division and realised that with reunion it would be impossible to carry on as before. Is this God's work? Not always easy to discern.

Any scheme for unity would require compromise from both sides and he recognised that the Church of England was already a coalition of compromises, of Catholic, Broad and Evangelical. Any service of reconciliation would need to provide for the ordination of Methodist Ministers. He did not want any reunification to hinder reunion with Rome and was aware that the Secretariat for Unity hoped for a successful outcome to Anglican-Roman Catholic conversations. There was one insuperable barrier that he could foresee to reunion with the Methodist church. His words were, no doubt, chosen carefully, and he did not commit himself in terms, when he commented that it would be "impossible for some Anglicans" to accept women Methodist Ministers who would be unable to be ordained. He had set out a series of questions and reservations that were voiced elsewhere in the Church of England. The division of opinion in Anglo-Catholicism

---

56   Parish Magazine June 1963.

was personified in the Bishop of Chichester, Dr Eric Kemp, who was in favour and the Bishop of Truro and, later, London, Dr Graham Leonard who was against.

Fr Roe had set out the questions and the boundaries of the discussion without committing himself.[57] But his position became perfectly clear within a few months when he expressed despondency and gloom at the favourable Norwich Diocesan Synod vote for the proposals. There was relief when the final vote failed to achieve the necessary two-thirds majority but the issue had taken a toll on him.

On one of the principal moral and social problems that characterised the cultural wars of the 1960s and 1970s but which, in particular, embroiled the Roman Catholic Church resonating beyond its denominational boundary, was that of the permissibility of artificial birth control, Fr Roe was more liberal than many Anglo-Catholics. On the publication of the Papal Encyclical *Humanae Vitae* he published an unusually long article in which he commented that "in spite of protestations that the document is inspired by great love and charity, it is obvious that it has been written by elderly and unmarried men with no personal experience of marriage." He went on, "As many of you know I am an ardent admirer of the present Pope [Paul VI] and of his personal holiness and devotion I have no doubt whatever. We look to the Pope for moral and spiritual guidance … but his advice is not always infallible." Rather, he commended the statement of the Lambeth Council 1958: "The means adopted to limit the number of children in a family are a matter for the consciences of each husband and wife. The use of artificial means of birth control is not excluded."[58]

His admiration for Pope John XXIII and Pope Paul VI may have spurred his interest in and attraction to the Focolare Movement. The Work of Mary, its formal title,[59] is an international Catholic

---

57   Parish Magazine August 1968.
58   Parish Magazine September 1968.
59   Under the formal name, Work of Mary, the organisation was approved in 1990 as an International Association of the Faithful of Political Right. Focolare, in Italian, means hearth or family fireside.

community inspired by the Gospel imperative for unity, to bring together all Christian traditions and world religions, even those with no formal faith. Non-catholics could also be members. It was founded in 1943 by Chiara Lubich in Trent, northern Italy. Central to its ethos, it was concerned, in its early days, with work in deprived areas. Members also met for summer vacations and retreats bringing priests and religious from various traditions to lead them. The Movement established a small house in Walsingham, presumably attracted more by the Roman Catholic Shrine and centuries of Marian devotion, rather than deprivation.[60] Here Fr Roe encountered them with encouragement from his Churchwarden, Robin Sayer, and his wife, Jan.

Early in his time in Walsingham, 1963, he was invited to give an address to a gathering of Focolare in Rome, where he had an audience with Pope John. As well as the Pope, he also met Cardinal Augustin Bea SJ, the first President of the Secretariat for Promoting Christian Unity, as well as Pope John's confessor. On his return Fr Roe spoke of the "love and devotion of a Christian community [that he had] never experienced completely before." He felt as though he had been present at a second Pentecost. It may have been statements such as this which seemed to have caused some unease amongst members of the congregation at his close association with the movement. In the movement, Fr Roe found an "almost inexpressible atmosphere of unity and charity, of complete and utter self-dedication to God and their fellow beings." Explaining the English translation of Focolare, hearth, he said that he felt "the heat and the fire of Christ ... the glowing embers of God's love."[61]

Later in the year he attended a second gathering, a summer conference where he gave an address, which was heard by the Apostolic Nuncio

---

60   It has not been possible to pinpoint the initial date for the establishment of a house but it may have been around 1962 when Chiara Lubich had a vision of creating permanent towns of members in simple houses, work places and schools.

61   Parish Magazine July 1963.

in the audience. Fr Roe later commented, seemingly approvingly, that the Mass was concelebrated facing the people, with little ceremonial and no music.[62] He returned to Focolare themes regularly for some years, writing frequently in the parish magazine. In 1966 he attended a conference in Rome during Holy Week, which included an audience with Pope Paul. He was the first to be presented and gave the Pope a statue of Our Lady of Walsingham.  He reported that Pope Paul had spoken to him of his hearing of "the great unity which existed in Walsingham amongst Catholics, Anglicans and Methodists" and gave Fr Roe a medal of SS Peter and Paul, emblazoned with the Papal Arms. He also met several members of the Curia.[63]

A month later he went to Trent to attend an ecumenical meeting. He imagined that he had been asked to speak to a small group of people from the parish but on arrival he found his name posted throughout the city. He was taken to a huge auditorium, holding some 1500 people, including the Archbishop of Trent. He spoke to them about the Church of England and of Walsingham. He recorded that his talk had been interrupted several times with applause and shouts of "bravissimo." Many shook his hand as they left.

He attended further ecumenical gatherings in 1965 and 1966. This last held in Sicily and, once again, he addressed a meeting of some thousand people in a large theatre, receiving a "deafening welcome." He spoke of the work of the Shrine, which elicited "tremendous applause." In a generous ecumenical gesture the Vicar General of the Diocese offered him an altar in the Cathedral to celebrate Mass.[64]

---

62 Parish Magazine September 1963.
63 Parish Magazine May 1966.
64 Parish Magazine October 1966.

A pilgrimage to Rome in May the following year, was to have been followed by a pilgrimage to Portugal and a conference in Avila but he was unable to go. After that, although he retained an interest in the movement and remained sympathetic, his direct involvement seems to have waned, and there is no record of further engagements. In part, this may have been influenced by some reservations in the parish about his involvement. Fr John Barnes sensed that the involvement had caused some division in the parish.[65]

Despite what some may have seen as a distraction, there seemed no diminution in parish meetings, social events, fund-raising activities as well as the round of pastoral visits, funerals, weddings, baptisms, confirmations, Lent courses, the commonplace long of all parish priests, as well as engagement with pilgrims to the Shrine.

Fr Roe had been inducted to the Living of Little Walsingham, along with which had also come responsibilities for Great Walsingham (S. Peter) and Houghton (S. Giles). These, however, had never been legally incorporated into one benefice. This was remedied in 1968. It gave Fr Roe the opportunity to reflect on the responsibilities of a parish priest. He wrote that his function as a parish priest was "not to be a curator of three museums who need to raise thousands of pounds to keep them standing up. My job is to look after people rather than maintain crumbling medieval buildings, however beautiful they may be." For good measure, he said that he was not a land-agent, museum keeper, or fund-raiser." I am not personally terribly interested in old buildings or works of art ... as far as I am concerned, as long as it is functional is sufficient ... but other people differ and to them antiquity and beauty are of major importance. Despite his personal feelings, however, he did his utmost to maintain the churches in his care in a reasonable condition and was fully engaged in the rebuilding of S. Mary's and insuring that its decoration and furnishings were of high quality

---

65   Fr John Barnes in correspondence.

and artistic merit. The rebarbative tone suggests some unhappiness, disappointment or lack of fulfilment during his time as Vicar.[66]

He had made a similar point two years earlier when he and his family had moved into the new (and present) vicarage. He had been happy to leave the old vicarage which had been enormous, set apart from the village, giving the impression to a modern generation that clergy had little to do with "working class folk." The new vicarage was modest in size but was still, unfortunately, on the edge of the village as no other site had been available.[67]

In this, as with the liturgical changes, Fr Roe was representative of his time. Change, reform was in the air. A new age, it was commonly thought, demanded new responses. He told his parishioners of the necessity for change. Pointing out, robustly and forthrightly, that some parishioners would only worship in one of the churches in the Benefice, or would only attend an early service of Holy Communion, he saw these "demands, [as] a kind of blackmail" for a parish priest felt bound to supply the needs of everybody. "Our outlook must change and we must move with the Church of the modern age." It was impossible to celebrate a Mass in every church on every Sunday.[68] It was vital for the whole benefice to join and worship together; if necessary making use of a minibus to travel to and from church. "Coming to Mass is not an individual affair … it is a corporate action." Not all these changes were dictated for theological or doctrinal reasons, nor to respond to the spirit of the age but because Fr Roe could not continue as before. He could not "manage on his own to say four Masses every Sunday, especially after illness."[69]

Fr Roe's health, periodically, was breaking down. He was absent

---

66   Fr John Barnes in correspondence.
67   Parish Magazine June 1966.
68   The revised Sunday timetable was Mass at S. Mary's 7.45 a.m. (moved from 8 a.m.: 1st and 3rd Sunday 8.30 a.m. Mass at S. Peter's. Mass at S. Mary's, the main benefice service at 11 a.m.. There was to be no Mass at S. Giles for the time being.
69   Parish Magazine November 1968.

from duty for two months, July and August 1969. On his 10th anniversary as parish priest, he wrote that, although he would not have missed his 10 years as parish priest, "it has been a strain ... a burnt out church, a lot of work rebuilding and raising money, a car crash, family illness [as well as] the day to day worries of priestly ministry."[70] The following year in January, on the 10th anniversary of the first publication of the parish magazine, he re-published his first letter adding in a footnote that little did he know what pain and anguish lay in store for him at the beginning of 1969. He had never lost his faith or felt that God had treated him unfairly, and accepted from God day to day, good and bad, good health and ill-health.

In 1970 he did not fare much better. His wife, Heather, underwent major surgery in February at S. Luke's Hospital for the Clergy, in London: the distance heightening his anxiety. On the Sunday after Corpus Christi, he collapsed during Mass and suffered a breakdown. Having suffered a coronary thrombosis in 1967 and rheumatic fever when he was in the Army, it began to be uncertain how long he could continue as parish priest. However, a hopeful prognosis from his doctors and a period of sick leave until late October saw a recovery and return to duty. In 1973, he spent a period in hospital under observation. He was absent from duties for three months in 1976, returning at the end of May but "still far from well." Two weeks later, it was announced that Fr Roe "had been taken away from the parish for the next week or so." Later that month he was given a further three months leave of absence. That proved insufficient to effect significant improvement and he announced to the PCC in September that he was to retire by the end of the year and would continue to be on leave of absence until then. Fr Carefull would be Acting Priest in Charge. "This early retirement is due entirely to ill-health over the past seven years and Fr Roe feels it not fair to the parishes to continue to have an

---

70   Parish Magazine August 1969.

ailing parish priest."[71] He and his family left the parish for a house in Colkirk in the following December.

For the next 14 years in Colkirk he did not return to any priestly ministry but he did return to live in Walsingham in his final years. In 1989, shortly after his appointment as Vicar, Fr Rear was informed that Fr Roe was seriously ill in hospital. He was not expected to survive the night. Fr Rear administered the Last Rites and sat for some time with Fr Roe, continuing to pray and talk to him, as Fr Roe seemed to hear. He survived the night and was able to return to his home in Colkirk. As his health continued to improve, he was invited by Fr Rear to return to S. Mary's along with Heather. As they had not been into S. Mary's since his resignation, their return was an emotional one. Further improvement meant that Fr Roe was able, with Fr Rear's persuasive encouragement, to return to public ministry and to concelebrate Mass. He further recovered his confidence enough to preach. He preached his first sermon for 14 years on Sunday, 29th July 1990. Fr Rear vividly recalled it as one of the most compelling and moving he had ever heard, "electrifying".[72] Fr Rear remembered Fr Roe being nervous at first but growing in confidence. He remembers it for being almost 30 minutes but the existing typescript is far shorter than that. There are details that Fr Rear remembers that are not in the text, and some are differently phrased. As many priests improvise when preaching, even with a script in front of them, and as Fr Roe found his public voice again and grew in confidence, it is highly likely that the combination of text and Fr Rear's eye-witness memory of it have the ring of truth and authenticity.

He spoke of his ill-health, physical and mental, with the mental anguish harder to bear than the physical.[73] He had suffered variously from Crohn's disease, heart attacks, prostate trouble, diabetes. But

---

71 PCC Minutes 26 September 1976
72 In correspondence and discussion.
73 The sources for this section are the typescript in the Parish Archive and Fr Rear's memories in correspondence and conversation.

also, in Fr Rear's recollection, serious depression and alcoholism, drinking a bottle of whisky a day. He had been in the care of one of the foremost psychiatrists of the day, Dr (later Sir) William Sargent at S. Thomas' Hospital in London. "I felt so ill, I wished I could die." He paid tribute to his wife "who had to find a menial job when I resigned to keep us solvent, [we were] penniless [with] nowhere to live." His wife, Heather, was an academic, having been a Science Lecturer at Reading University. She was unable to secure a teaching post at Fakenham High School without a Post Graduate Certificate of Education qualification. She became a laboratory technician.

Through the depths of his illness, however dark the days, he maintained his priestly discipline of saying Mass at home and saying the Daily Office, as much as was physically and mentally possible. As a result of his trials, he was a "more fervent Christian." In a passage of his sermon which referred to the Precious Blood in the Mass, he said that "Grapes, unless they are crushed, cannot produce wine." Fr Rear, however, remembered it as "Grapes have to be crushed to provide wine," which struck him forcibly then as obviously powerfully self-referential. "He spoke loudly and emphatically about his faith God and God's constant mercy to him."[74] The personal nature of the sermon, almost an exorcism of demons, a release from the tribulations of the recent past, and the return to Walsingham seem to show that he had reached a safe haven having come through stormy, tempestuous waters.

He and Heather bought a bungalow in Cleaves Drive, with Fr Rear's encouragement.[75] He was able to cover when Fr Rear took his holiday and re-connected with many of the parishioners whom he had known as Vicar and whom he felt that he had neglected during the years of his ill-health.

Fr Roe was not able to enjoy this last, contented phase for long. At

---

74 Fr Rear in correspondence.
75 It is not customary for a priest in retirement to live in the parish where he had served as Incumbent.

the Dedication Mass of the Sisters of S. Margaret, in the convent, Fr Roe was saying the Bidding Prayers and when he came to the prayers for the departed Sisters by name, "he suddenly stopped speaking and [Fr Rear] saw him jerk into the air before dropping down, dead."[76] Fr Roe died on 12th May 1992. He was 66. His ashes were buried in the churchyard next to the grave of Fr Patten.

---

76   Fr Rear in correspondence.

JOHN EDGAR BARNES

Fr John Edgar Barnes was inducted to the Living on 3rd May 1977. He was born in Chester in 1945. His parents were active members of their parish church. His father was Churchwarden and his mother ran the junior Sunday School, "somewhat unconventionally, but with flair and success,"[77] in a middle-of-the road parish. At about 12 years of age, he decided that he would like to be a clergyman. His youthful reading of the Barchester Chronicles by Anthony Trollope may have had an influence but he had also concluded that the life of an Anglican clergyman was "reasonably comfortable and secure." Not necessarily an ignoble aspiration but, Fr Barnes wrote that "my motives were definitely dubious … I liked comfort and security. Not good motives for seeking ordination, but I simply knew no better at that time. I think grace is very adept at purifying our motives over time."[78]

Academically a late-developer, having failed his 11+ examination, he attended a secondary modern school but, having passed several O Levels, he transferred to Chester City Grammar School where, following two years in the 6th Form, he passed five A Level examinations. He read Theology and Philosophy at S. David's College, Lampeter, then a constituent college of the University of Wales. He graduated in 1966. Here, in the Church in Wales, he first encountered Anglo-Catholicism. From Lampeter he gravitated to the North-East of England to undertake post-graduate study at Durham University, as a member of S. Chad's College, with its established Anglo-Catholic ethos. He obtained a Master's degree for his work on Anglican theology of the 17th century. His sense of priestly vocation had continued to develop and he was accepted for ordination training by his home diocese of Chester.

---

77   Fr Barnes in correspondence.
78   Fr Barnes in correspondence.

He was, however, rather dismayed that before going to theological college, the diocese required him to spend a year in industry. This was the kind of relevant work experience that the Church of England, ever on trend, required of its prospective ordinands. A sympathetic archdeacon, however, permitted him to spend a year in alternative employment. He taught in a Preparatory School in the Malvern Hills, which, shades of Evelyn Waugh, seemed like a 1920s time-warp. His A Level Art qualification was sufficient for him to be the Art Master. From there he went to S. Stephen's House in Oxford to prepare for ordination. He also became a member of Oriel College which would enable him to submit a dissertation, not subsequently completed, for the degree of Bachelor of Divinity, a post-graduate qualification.[79]

He was ordained deacon in S. Nicholas' Cathedral, Newcastle upon Tyne to serve his title at S. John Baptist, Grainger Street; a few hundred yards from the Cathedral, near the Central Railway Station. In the following year, he was ordained to the priesthood. S. John's was the leading Anglo-Catholic parish in a traditionally high-church diocese. Between the Wars it had been significantly influential in the Parish Communion movement under its then Vicar, Noël Baring Hudson[80] and his curate, Henry de Candole.[81] After World War II city-centre slum clearance had left the parish with only a handful of resident parishioners but many former residents continued to travel into the city centre from the suburbs and the housing estates on the outskirts of the city. The principal Sunday services were the 9:15 a.m. Parish Communion, followed by High Mass at 11 a.m.

The Vicar under whom Fr Barnes served was Fr Alan Carefull. From a wealthy Liverpool family and of independent means, Fr Carefull had been trained at S. Stephen's House and before coming to S. John's had been Vice Principal of the House. He was rigorously

---

79   Registration for the BD degree ceased in 2005.
80   1893-1970. Awarded DSO and MC during World War I. 1922-1931 Vicar S. John Baptist; 1931-1938 Bishop of Labuan and Sarawak; 1941-1957 Bishop of Newcastle; 1957-1961 Bishop of Ely.
81   1895-1971. 1949-1965 Bishop of Knaresborough.

self-disciplined and required the same standards from his curates. Strong in his opinions, with great strength of character, rigorous and forceful, he significantly influenced Fr Barnes and, later, played a part in his appointment to Walsingham. In his three years as curate Fr Barnes came to love Tyneside and Northumberland. However, Fr Carefull moved to Walsingham to become the Administrator of the Shrine. He was succeeded by a married man and the Clergy House, shared by Fr Carefull and his two curates, became a vicarage. Fr Barnes moved to his second curacy.

He was appointed to S. Asaph in 1973 to be Vicar Choral in the Cathedral and Curate of S. Asaph with Tremeirchion. The Dean, Raymond Renowden, had taught Fr Barnes philosophy at Lampeter. Although this was never realised, the Dean intended to establish a Study Centre at the Cathedral and Fr Barnes went to assist in that project. He spent four years as Minor Canon and Curate of the Parish Church. His work concentrated on ministry among the young and he became Chaplain to Lowther College, a girls' public school. In 1977 he went to spend his post-Christmas break in Walsingham with Fr Carefull who told him that Fr Roe had retired through ill-health and that John Gurney, as Patron, was having difficulty finding a replacement. Somewhat in desperation, not sharing Fr Carefull's churchmanship, Mr Gurney asked if he knew of anyone who might be suitable. Fr Carefull was able to tell him that a young priest staying with him was ready to move from his curacy and invited Mr Gurney to see Fr Barnes. An interview followed. It now sounds quaintly eccentric compared to current bureaucratic practice but, in its way, sufficiently rigorous and intuitive.

Fr Barnes remembered: "Mr Gurney asked whether I had a photograph of my parents with me. I had not. The first bad mark. Then he asked if I knew the Bible. Not such an easy question as it sounds. I said yes, I suppose I did. "Well who then," he continued, "were Huppin, Muppin, and Ard?" I did not know. Another bad mark. "I thought you knew the Bible," he said accusingly.[82] Things were going badly but suddenly the tide changed. I was asked what my maternal grandfather had done for a living, and when I said that he had owned a fishmongers' shop in Chester, that was thought to be highly relevant and advantageous. And then the *coup de grace*: I was asked what my A Level subjects were, and when I mentioned Art he leapt from the table and shouted upstairs to his wife "Anne! Anne! He did Art!" I was duly appointed Vicar of Walsingham."[83]

Fr Barnes had struck a chord, said the right thing. Mr Gurney owned and ran the Medici Society. It had been founded in 1908 by Philip Lee-Warner and Eustace Gurney. The business was run as a society, and members were invited to join and pay a subscription which entitled them to copies of prints as they were published at no extra charge. This structure was later revised and the prints were sold commercially through shops and galleries. The company still retains the Medici Society name. Although Mr and Mrs Gurney did not share Fr Barnes' churchmanship, the Gurneys being a Norwich family of long-standing evangelical sympathy, they proved to be kind, generous, helpful and hospitable Patrons. They often carried out their charitable giving anonymously, "doing good by stealth."[84] They made several such contributions to the parish and church causes during Fr Barnes' time there.

They did not worship in S. Mary's, having been "driven away by Fr Patten's high-church practices." They travelled to Great and Little Snoring to attend church. However, on occasion they would attend the Eucharist at Houghton S. Giles. There were a few eccentric quirks. Invariably late arriving at Houghton, Mr Gurney would search for a Book of Common Prayer, never found, and there would be the

---

82   The Bishop of S. Asaph later told Fr Barnes that they were the sons of Benjamin. (Genesis 46:21) Their names had been used for the title of a tract on religious education written by Mr Gurney's distinguished Anglo-Catholic uncle, Samuel Gurney.

83   Fr Barnes in correspondence.

84   Fr Barnes in correspondence.

occasional loud aside to his wife about the Vicar's audibility, despite the fact that Fr Barnes' clarity of diction and audibility were obvious to all. Fr Barnes considered Mr Gurney to be under-appreciated for maintaining the character and the attractiveness of the village. Shrewd and successful businessman that he was, he could have followed trends elsewhere by selling land, renting cottages to holiday-makers or similar schemes. At the time there were still several small, family businesses in the villages and a number of long-standing locals born and bred in the village. Mr Gurney was determined to maintain the traditional character of the village and of village life. They were also generous in allowing the Abbey grounds to be used for church events.

The task facing Fr Barnes was neither an easy nor a straightforward one. Inevitably and sadly, the periodic bouts of ill-health that afflicted his predecessor had a deleterious effect on the life of the parish, despite efforts to maintain its life and routines. Much of its life had been sustained by the parish officers and by Fr Stephenson providing cover, and, later, by Fr Carefull during the Interregnum. Yet, unavoidably, there had been a degree of stasis, even "stagnation."[85] There was also an element of division and unease over the degree of Fr Roe's involvement in the Focolare movement, that needed to be addressed. Further, S. Giles' church, Houghton had been closed for 10 years and S. Peter's in Great Walsingham "had a very neglected air, and a service was held there only every other week."[86] After his first two months in post Fr Barnes wrote that he had appreciated the "friendliness" of his welcome but had noticed "how little impact the Church is making on village life." There was a small number who were regular communicants but "hardly any penitents."[87]

In his early 30s, Fr Barnes brought to his new task much energy and enthusiasm. He quickly restored a daily Mass to S. Mary's, suspended

---

85 Fr Christopher Colven in correspondence.
86 Fr Barnes in correspondence.
87 Walsingham Monthly Journal July 1977.

during the Interregnum, and restored a weekly Sunday Mass at S. Peter's at 9 a.m. Later, he offered a further weekly Mass on Fridays at 10.30 a.m. Within a short time of his arrival he re-opened S. Giles' church. It took some hard work with a team to remove 10 years of dust and dirt. He instituted a weekly Sunday Mass at 10 a.m. Both churches required structural attention. At S. Giles' the roof of the tower needed to be renewed, and a new weathercock, donated by a local GP, erected. Inside pendant lighting was installed, acquired from Seascale Church in Cumbria. An annual Carol Service was begun which became a valued feature of parish life. Fortunately, it was a time when government grants were available and they enabled S. Peter's tower to be re-roofed and other fabric to be renewed. S Peter's became the host for the annual Harvest Festival Service followed by a Harvest Supper. Fr Barnes worked closely with Brian Landale at S. Peter's, despite their difference of churchmanship. There was a mutual regard between the Anglo-Catholic and the Ulster Protestant. Fr Barnes regarded him as "good and faithful … gracious and generous."[88] Brian Landale thought Fr Barnes "a thoroughly nice man [with a] sense of humour."[89]

As S. Mary's had been re-built following the fire, there was no need for any substantial structural work, only minor repairs and maintenance being necessary. Released from these constraints, which so often bedevil parishes and incumbents, Fr Barnes was able to make a considerable contribution to beautifying and enhancing the interior of the church. A temporary window was replaced on the south side of the Chancel. The Norwich glazier Dennis King installed three new lights bordered by fragments of medieval glass. Through his acquaintance with Fr Anthony Symondson SJ, the noted art historian and expert on the work of Sir Ninian Comper,[90] Fr Barnes was able to obtain a reredos for the church's Guilds' Chapel from the Community

---

88   Fr Barnes in correspondence.
89   Brian Landale in conversation.
90   See Anthony Symondson and Stephen Bucknall, Sir Ninian Comper: An introduction to his life and work with complete gazetteer. Spire Books & the Ecclesiological Society. Reading & London [2006].

of S. Andrew, Westbourne Park, London. It was then believed to be Comper's earliest recorded work. Fr Barnes thought that its installation in S. Mary's would be an ideal complement to the Comper reredos in the Holy House of the Shrine, one of his last commissions. Fr Barnes engaged the conservator Peter Larkworthy of Baldock to renovate the reredos from the amateur and hideous repainting by the S. Andrew's Deaconesses. Peter Larkworthy had already restored the Achievement of Arms on the Sidney tombs at the west of the church and he completed a similar sensitive restoration of the reredos. A short time after its installation, Fr Symondson revised his original opinion, having realised that he had misread a diary entry of Comper's and decided that the reredos was not the work of Comper but of G. F. Bodley.[91]

Another major undertaking was re-hanging the bells. S. Mary's housed the heaviest ring of five in Norfolk but the decay of the wooden medieval bell-frame meant that the bells had not been heard for a century or more. On the advice of the Whitechapel Bell Foundry, the bells could only be heard if the rotten oak medieval frame was replaced with a metal frame. Although by instinct a conservationist, Fr Barnes was convinced that the bells should ring again. Generous donations, some by stealth, and a legacy allowed the replacement of the wooden frame and rehanging the bells, plus a sixth bell. This was baptised Francis and Fr Barnes wrote the inscription, "My name is Francis / Loud I'll ring / For Mary / Mother of my King."

Fr Barnes was particularly glad to welcome the return of the alabaster statue of the Immaculate Conception that had been damaged by the fire, discarded and rescued from a rubbish dump. As the statue pre-dated the arrival of Fr Patten, and had marked the first time Mary returned to Walsingham since the Reformation, he determined that it should enjoy a prominent position in church and become the focus for devotion to Our Lady, especially during May, Mary's month.

---

91   Fr Barnes in correspondence. Fortunately Bodley, was also a favourite of Fr Barnes.

Throughout the month the statue was flanked by candles and had banks of flowers in front. After Mass on Sunday there was a procession to the statue where the *Regina Coeli* or the *Angelus* was sung.

Liturgically Fr Barnes was not a papalist and did not use material from Roman Catholic liturgical resources. He believed that as an Anglican he ought to use authorised Anglican rites. In 1980 the PCC resolved to use Rite A, the modern language Communion Rite, of the ASB (nine votes to four).[92] The Creed was to be said, not sung, at the Parish Mass. This, he argued, was decided in accordance with the "general practice of the Church." The Creed was neither a hymn of praise, nor a prayer but "a solemn profession of belief…a statement of faith" and as a commonly held and professed statement of faith the appropriate usage should be the *We believe* form rather than *I believe*. "Faith is not a matter of private judgement."[93] In 1981 he conducted a consultation by questionnaire about the Sunday morning liturgy. He reminded parishioners that it was the duty of the parish priest to determine liturgical use but as the Anglican way was to consult rather than to impose, he invited comment.

Opinion was "fairly evenly divided" on using the high altar, eastward facing, or a free-standing nave altar, facing the people. Fr Barnes was among those who did not prefer one over the other but, on balance, it was decided to keep the free-standing altar consonant with the current practice of Western Christendom, celebrating the family meal. A majority favoured a sung, rather than a said, Gospel as giving added dignity. There was a large majority against the laity having a part in the Intercessions, many on practical grounds of audibility, "riding hobby-horses," or length. Respondents were equally divided over the desirability of an Offertory Procession. Strong feelings, both for and against, were expressed about the young singing during the distribution of Holy Communion. A large majority welcomed the attendance and participation of Shrine pilgrims. Such

---

92   Walsingham Monthly Journal December 1980.
93   Walsingham Monthly Journal October 1980.

quasi-democratic exercises have their limitation but are of some use in providing a snapshot of the life of a parish, its attitudes, likes, dislikes, foibles, qualities.

Fr Barnes' graduate studies of 17th century Caroline Divines, his time at both S. John Baptist, Newcastle and S. Asaph Cathedral influenced and shaped a more Anglican Catholicism, English rather than Roman liturgical expression. It was also helpful in distinguishing the parish church from the Shrine. The relationship between the two had not been fully resolved since the death of Fr Patten. Tensions had remained. These were institutional rather than personal, although Fr Roe had felt himself in the shadow of Fr Stephenson. They were two institutions in a small village with clienteles that overlapped but were, in essence, different. There had to be a *modus vivendi.*

The long-standing relationship between Fr Barnes and Fr Carefull made for a better working relationship between parish church and Shrine. As Fr Carefull's curate, Fr Barnes had been given a degree of independent responsibility and leeway in his work that made it highly unlikely there would be something akin to a curate/vicar relationship now they were both working in Walsingham.[94] Fr Barnes maintained a position of cooperation without being seen as under the wing of the Shrine, nor an adjunct to it. The integrity of the parish was important and it was his concern to breathe life back into it. He had youth on his side and the energetic commitment to effect revival. While it was possible to argue that Walsingham was a country parish, it was not an ordinary country parish. The Shrine could not be ignored. Pilgrims to the Shrine also came to the parish church and engaged, however briefly and sporadically, in the everyday life of the parish that was not encountered to anything like the same extent elsewhere.

Fr Carefull was succeeded by Fr Christopher Colven and a different relationship was required. He was the same age as Fr Barnes and was

---

94   Fr Barnes had been in the Clergy House when Fr Carefull collapsed with a ruptured aorta. He spent much of his convalescence in Walsingham during which paved the way for him becoming Administrator.

much more oriented towards a Roman and papalist expression of Anglo-Catholicism. He and Fr Barnes lunched in the College together every week and co-operated where possible and appropriate, having established a cordial, business-like working relationship.

The parish and its integrity were foremost for Fr Barnes. He was not single-handed and was able to call upon a number of able and committed laity. Prominent among them was Robin Sayer who was a "loyal, faithful … devout" Churchwarden, a Guardian, and his wife Jan. Both had been influenced by the Focolare movement. He was succeeded as Churchwarden by Major Patrick King who was equally loyal and hardworking and, as a Guardian, also provided a link with the Shrine. As did Stanley Smith, Churchwarden and Treasurer, as well as Guardian and Bursar of the Shrine who was "unflappable, humorous, seemingly omni-competent." For many years, before and after Fr Barnes he was completely reliable and a stalwart of parish life. Fr Barnes commented that "we all relied upon him … he never let us down."[95]

There was a cohort of formidable retired ladies who had moved to the village to be near to the Shrine, to which they were devoted, as also to the memory of Fr Patten. Fr Carefull referred to them as "the resident company." Fr Barnes felt that the Shrine devotees never quite approved of him. There were "two leading ladies, who lived almost next-door-but-one to each other in Knight Street [and] viewed each other with circumspection."[96] One was the Hon. Elise Coke, widowed daughter-in-law of the 3rd Earl of Leicester (of Holkham Hall). She was "very devout, plucky and lavishly hospitable."[97] Small, plump, she loved her food (her father was French) and men but despised women. She drove, peering just above the steering wheel, a yellow (the Coke family livery colour) Renault 4.

---

95 Fr Barnes in correspondence.
96 Fr Barnes in correspondence
97 Elsewhere Fr Barnes, as a guest of another parishioner, had once been invited by his host to carve a pheasant between six.

Enid Chadwick was renowned as the Shrine artist and had been closely associated with Fr Patten: her work remains much admired. Fr Barnes, once an Art Master, and with a very good eye and keen artistic appreciation found her art "charming and child-like" but only two dimensional. Her work which was invariably "innocent and joyous … did not entirely match her character." Querulous, sharp, acidic, she often read a novel during sermons, although on one occasion she congratulated Fr Barnes, "I liked your sermon last Sunday, you're usually so boring." He wondered, but did not ask, how she knew. Once summoned to her sick bed in the busy period leading to Christmas, he was a little late for his appointment with her to receive orders about setting up the Crib, which was her domain, she greeted him, "I should have thought you could have been on time when you're doing the Lord's work."[98] They were, however, fond of each other in their way and did attend together the Loughborough Conference on Catholic Renewal in 1978. The PCC was asked whether they should attend as representatives of the parish but this was "not looked on with favour."[99]

Fr Barnes enjoyed a more satisfactory relationship with the Sisters of S. Margaret, then from the Priory of Our Lady, Sisters of Margaret, the East Grinstead Sisters. Under Mother Julian, the Sisters proved highly effective and were much loved in the parish as well as with pilgrims to the Shrine. He used to conduct a Holy Hour for them once a week, Mother Julian invariably falling asleep within minutes, and he lunched with them on Saturdays. He entertained the Sisters and their Roman Catholic counterparts, the Little Sisters of Jesus, an order inspired by the life and writings of Charles de Foucauld, priest, hermit and martyr, during the Christmas Octave, for Afternoon Tea and carols.

Fr Barnes was particularly eager to develop work with children and young people in the parish and he paid a good deal of attention to that

98   Fr Barnes in correspondence.
99   PCC Minutes February 1978.

ministry. He enlisted Sister Clare and Sister Wendy to assist. Sister Clare had a keen interest in and an affinity with children, being herself child-like in her approach and always cheerful. The highlights for her and for the girls were the festivities of Corpus Christi, when the girls, dressed in white, scattered rose petals, and the Assumption when they scattered herbs. Sister Wendy sang and accompanied herself on the guitar and would play, after a regular display of reluctance, at many children's events.

A Saturday morning club was initiated shortly after his arrival in the parish. Mass at 10 a.m. in the Guilds' Chapel was followed by various activities in the south porch, ending with a game. Between 15-20 children regularly attended. There was also a Children's Mission, known in the village as the Holiday Club, usually of four days during summer when numbers would rise to between 40-50. Ordinands on summer placement from S. Stephen's House would sometimes assist. There would be a coach trip, usually to Cromer. Despite his enthusiasm for the ministry to children, Fr Barnes was unable to penetrate the village school to take an Assembly or to offer religious instruction. Although the Headmaster's mother was a faithful worshipper at S. Peter's and the Headmaster himself was a member of the Men's Group, and held a Christmas Carol Service in S. Mary's, he was adamant in his refusal to admit Fr Barnes to the school in his official capacity. Only when a more amenable and eager successor was appointed was it possible but by then Fr Barnes was in his last weeks in the parish.

The Men's Group, inaugurated by Fr Barnes, who arranged the meetings, met monthly in the Black Lion Hotel. Attendance was usually about a dozen, not all with a church connection. There was a speaker, followed by a discussion and conversation. A wide range of topics and interests was covered, usually non-religious in content. In the three summer months, evening outings replaced the usual monthly meetings at the Black Lion. The September meeting, to which wives were invited, comprised a Mass in S. Mary's followed by supper in the vicarage. This was a contribution to the common life of the village rather than overtly church related.

There was a range of further activities in church and in the life of the village that was part of the parish priest's work and engagement. There was a branch of the Mothers' Union, which had a monthly Corporate Communion, a Young Communicants' Group, which, as well as its regular meetings in Walsingham, had one weekend a year away. There was an annual Flower Festival at Houghton which attracted much interest and a Parish Retreat. Fr Barnes was keen to have a Parish Mission in 1986 conducted by Fr Augustine Hoey CR, who had conducted one in Fr Patten's time, aimed at committed Christians, lapsed members, other interested people but the PCC voted against it and the idea was dropped.[100]

Fr Patten had made the Assumption of Our Lady, 15th August, the Patronal Festival of the church. Its observation had been relatively muted in the recent past and Fr Barnes aimed to revive it and add to it. There would continue to be a Sung Mass on the evening of the Feast followed by a barbecue and a fireworks display in the garden of the house opposite the church. However, Fr Barnes thought that the liturgical and social celebrations ought to be balanced and complemented by some Marian theology, and decided to extend the celebration to earlier in the day. He conceived the idea of an annual lecture on a Marian theme to be called the Assumptiontide Lecture. To inaugurate it as a serious contribution to the parish and to the wider church, and to secure a base for its continuation, he realised that the standard should be set by a distinguished lecturer from the first. He could not have found any better than Fr Eric Mascall.

Along with Austin Farrar and Dom. Gregory Dix, he was one of the most influential and outstanding Anglican theologians of the 20th century. A prolific author and wit, he had taught at Lincoln

---

100 PCC Minutes 9 September 1985.

Theological College and Christ Church, Oxford. He retired in 1973 as Professor of Historical Theology at King's College, London, and resided in the Clergy House of S. Mary, Bourne Street. He launched the series with a lecture entitled, "The Centrality of Mary."[101] It was the beginning of a distinguished series which continues today and is an abiding legacy of Fr Barnes' foresight. Fr Edward (Ted) Yarnold SJ of Campion Hall, Oxford, lectured the following year. He was followed by, Professor John Maquarrie, Canon Donald Allchin, Canon Cheslyn Jones, former Principal of Pusey House, Fr David Hope, then Vicar of All Saints' Margaret Street and Dr Graham Leonard. He was Bishop of London and widely regarded as the leader of the Anglo-Catholic Movement. As he entered the packed church with Fr Barnes, the members of the audience "all stood up and broke into spontaneous applause." [102]

Beyond the parish, Fr Barnes became the Secretary of the Diocesan Advisory Committee for the Care of Churches (later becoming its Chairman). He could draw on his early experience during his curacy in Newcastle when Stephen Dykes-Bower re-ordered S. John Baptist church.[103] Most of his work was congenial as he had an early interest in historic buildings from childhood. As well as dealing with the substantial paperwork generated, he also visited many churches throughout the diocese to give advice and guidance on proposed works or schemes of restoration, renovation, or precautions against potential acts of vandalism. It also enabled him to enjoy the company and share the expertise of Committee members including Lady ("Billa") Harrod, Lord Walpole, the artist John Maddison and the architect Neil Birdsall. His work on the Committee and its concern

---

101 To indicate his support, he returned the following year to hear the lecture of his successor.
102 Fr Barnes in correspondence.
103 Fr Carefull would not apply for a Faculty, refusing to submit the designs of such a distinguished architect for the consideration of such an undistinguished DAC. He waited for the DAC to ask him to accept a Faculty, which they did.

with consecrated church buildings was conducted from what he regarded as the "regrettable box-like and graceless new vicarage redeemed only by its charming views across parkland." Perhaps his aversion caused him on one occasion to lock himself out. One of his confirmation class took a wire coat-hanger from her home, fashioned it into a hook and, by way of the cat-flap, recovered the keys from the worktop of the utility room where he had left them.[104]

It was the Chairman of the Committee, Canon David Bishop, who encouraged Fr Barnes to stage a series of exhibitions of contemporary art in S. Mary's. One of the exhibitors, Naomi Blake, donated a statue of a Mother and Child, which she had sculpted, to the church. Other exhibitions included one of works by a Carmelite Nun from Quiddenham, and one by the clergy of the diocese of paintings.

Canon Bishop was also helpful when the parish received a small legacy which Fr Barnes wished to use to commission a piece of contemporary art. Canon Bishop put him in touch with a friend of his, the Chairman of the Arts Council of Great Britain, Peter Palumbo. He flew into Walsingham by helicopter, landing in the meadow beyond the vicarage, which had been cleared of cows by the farmer. He looked at the niche leading up to S. Catherine's Chapel which Fr Barnes had identified as the appropriate setting, proposed an American ceramicist, whom he then commissioned, and flew her over from America to make a series of maquettes. All the costs were borne by Lord Palumbo.

Rather less enjoyable was Fr Barnes' membership of the General Synod of the Church of England as a Prolocutor in Convocation. He was motivated by the movement for the ordination of women which was gaining momentum and becoming a significant issue in Synod and beyond. Pressure was growing for legislation in the Synod. Fr Barnes believed passionately that the proposals were contrary to Catholic ministerial order and the unbroken teaching of the Church. Ordination of women to the priesthood, and it logically followed, to

---

104 Lynette Sutton in correspondence.

the episcopate would invalidate the claims of the Church of England to catholicity. He had also been opposed to the Anglican-Methodist Covenant because it would allow women ministers into episcopal ministry and would be a stumbling-block in relations with the Roman Catholic Church and the Eastern Orthodox Churches.[105] He attended Synod meetings in London and York "hating every minute" of the factional disputes and the ill-feeling they generated.

Although Fr Barnes recognised Fr Patten's significance, he found his cult status a little oppressive and thought that he unduly overshadowed Fr Woodward, whose Anglo-Catholicism pre-dated that of Fr Patten. Fr Woodward had been a writer of hymns and carols, *Ding dong! Merrily on high* and *This Joyful Eastertide* among them. He had supported Fr Patten's work and had become a Priest Associate of the Holy House. Fr Barnes visited surviving relatives and collected material for a biography that was published after he left Walsingham.[106] While still Incumbent, he published *Ghost Stories of a Norfolk Parson*[107] They were fictional but based in Walsingham, disguised as Wennington. He also contributed a pamphlet on Fr Patten to the series published by the Church Union to celebrate the sesquicentenary of the Oxford Movement in 1983.

Unexpectedly, after 12 years in Walsingham and having begun to sense that a change might be beneficial to him and the parish, he was telephoned by the Bishop of Norwich who asked him to take the Living of Wymondham. As a man under authority, Fr Barnes agreed. As he put down the telephone, he wept.[108] He was able to leave Walsingham having achieved much as a faithful parish priest. He was "the epitome

---

105 PCC Minutes 23 October 1981.
106 George Ratcliffe Woodward 1848-1934 Priest, Poet and Musician. Norwich, The Canterbury Press [1995].
107 Published by Continuum (Mowbray Leisure Series).
108 Fr Barnes wrote that the Bishop "explained that there had been a crisis there, and that he wanted to appoint a new incumbent from within the diocese. He had been … all through the clergy list, and the only person available seemed to be me. Rather a back-handed compliment."

of a parish priest: wholly committed to his people, gifted, gentle, everything that one could ask from a pastor. Pope Francis' phrase about the pastor knowing the smell of the sheep, would apply."[109]

Following the decision of General Synod in 1994 to admit women to the priesthood, Fr Barnes resigned and was received into the Roman Catholic Church. He was successively Assistant Priest in Lowestoft (1995-1996), Parish Priest in Bury St Edmunds (1996-2001), East Dereham (2001-2014) and is currently serving in Felixstowe.

---

109 Fr Christopher Colven in correspondence. In his Holy Thursday Homily given in S. Peter's Rome 2013 Pope Francis said that priests should be "shepherds living with the smell of the sheep."

MICHAEL JOHN REAR

F'r Michael John Rear was inducted to the Living on 4th August 1989, the Feast of the Curé d'Ars (S. Jean Vianney, patron of parish priests), and the anniversary of the surrender of Walsingham Abbey to the agents of King Henry VIII. Fr Rear was among the first priests to be appointed to a Living under a new system of patronage. General Synod had passed the Patronage (Benefices) Measure in 1986 and it had come into operation on 1st January 1989. This new procedure limited the hitherto unfettered rights of the patron to present to the Living[110] and now included the parish in the choice of its own parish priest. The PCC had to draw up a parish profile and could request, within certain constraints, the qualities it would prefer in a candidate. Once the patron had chosen the preferred candidate, two elected parish representatives (each of whom had a veto) had to agree, as, subsequently, had the bishop. One of the stipulations made by the Walsingham and Houghton PCC was that the new priest should be under 50 years of age. At 49½ Fr Rear qualified. Unknown to him, someone submitted his name, and he found himself one of 14 'applicants', of whom 4 were shortlisted.[111] Fr Rear recalled that Stanley Smith, Churchwarden and one of the Parish Representatives asked only one question, and that Fr Rear thought was the crucial one: could he sing? He could.[112]

Fr Rear was born in 1940 in Louth, Lincolnshire and spent his first few months in Binbrook, where his father and mother owned a shop and café. Binbrook became an air base during the War and Fr Rear was brought up in Doncaster, his mother's home town. He

---

110 The patron, (the Crown, an individual, the bishop, or an institution) owns the advowson, the right of presentation. It is, in law, property, albeit a "peculiar piece of property".

111 Annual Meeting Report 1989.

112 Fr Rear in correspondence.

was baptised in Christ Church and there learned the Catholic faith. Its Vicar, Fr Francis Frazer, had incurred episcopal displeasure and was "under the ban" for giving Benediction once a year on the Feast of Corpus Christi. Consequently, Fr Rear was confirmed in S. Wilfrid's, Cantley by the Bishop of Sheffield, Dr Leslie Hunter. When Fr Rear was in his mid-teens the then Vicar of Christ Church, Fr Sayers, decided that Fr Rear should see the Bishop about becoming an ordinand. There was an early opportunity because Bishop Hunter was due to preach at Doncaster Congregational chapel. In an early foretaste of Fr Rear's firm principles, he declined to meet the Bishop at a "schismatic conventicle." They met elsewhere and the eirenic Bishop Hunter agreed to sponsor him to go, in due course, to a Selection Conference.

After secondary school, Fr Rear joined the Civil Service and went south to work. He lived in Notting Hill, partly because, before gentrification, accommodation was cheap to rent, and partly so that he could be part of the congregation at All Saints' Notting Hill under its parish priest, Fr Twisaday,[113] also a Guardian of the Shrine. He took a friendly interest in Fr Rear. From childhood Fr Rear had a sense of vocation to the priesthood which continued to be fostered in the parish, with the support of Fr Twisaday. The next staging post on the way to ordination was to spend a year in Durham at the Bernard Gilpin Society. Here he followed a course of study designed to prepare students for Theological College. As well as theology, the course, which he successfully completed, also included the study of philosophy and law. It was while in Durham that he met his future wife Catherine, Cathy, who was training to be a teacher.

He studied for the priesthood at Lichfield Theological College. He had chosen Lichfield partly because a curate in his parish in Doncaster had trained there, and partly because it had been Fr Patten's college. John Fenton, later Canon of Christ Church, Oxford, was the Principal. In Fr Rear's final year, he was offered the opportunity to

---

113 John Herbert Cloete Twisaday.

study at the Ecumenical Institute at Bossy, near Geneva, run by the World Council of Churches. With no burning desire to spend time in Calvin's redoubt, he suggested, rather boldly, to John Fenton that he would be more interested in studying in Rome. His presumption was rewarded with a year in Rome, in the midst of the Second Vatican Council, as the first of a line of Anglican ordinands spending a year of study in Rome. He lived with the Rosminian Fathers[114] at St John before the Latin Gate. Some years later he was told that the Rector had informed staff and students that a young Anglican student would be staying with them, sharing their life and going with them to the Gregorian University. They were under strict instructions not to try to convert him. Attending lectures at the Gregorian enabled him to hear the leading theologians of the day: Fr Charles Boyer SJ[115], Dom. Edward Schillebeeckx OP[116], Fr Gustave Weigel SJ[117], Fr Bernard Häring CSsR[118], Hans Kung[119] and Fr Louis Bouyer Cong. Orat.[120] Fr Bouyer took him to meet Pope Paul VI, who enquired where he was to be ordained. On being told 'York Minster' Pope Paul told him he had been there and that it was very beautiful. He also asked him to convey

---

114 The Institute of Charity.

115 Professor at the Gregorian University. Authority on S. Augustine of Hippo.

116 One of the most active and controversial theologians of the modern era. Based at the University of Nijmegan, he published extensively and was under scrutiny three times by the Congregation for the Doctrine of the Faith but never condemned.

117 Advocated the adoption by the Vatican Council of a statement absolving Jews of blame for the Crucifixion of Jesus and calling for better relations between the Catholic Church and the Jewish people. He was an adviser to the Secretariat for the Promotion of Christian Unity, under Augustin, Cardinal Bea.

118 Redemptorist. Moral Theologian. Advisor to the Vatican Council not least on the pastoral constitution *Gaudium et Spes*.

119 Professor (now Emeritus) University of Tübingen. Although no longer officially allowed to teach Catholic theology, his priestly faculties have not been removed.

120 Born a Lutheran but converted to Roman Catholicism. Advisor to Vatican II.

his blessing to his parish. These were heady days for an Anglican ordinand, stimulating and formative.

On his return to England and on the successful completion of his training, he was ordained to the diaconate in York Minster to serve his title as curate of S. Alban, Hull. On his first Sunday he conveyed the Pope's blessing as he had been asked to do. His training Incumbent was Fr Douglas Carter, who was later appointed General Secretary of the Church Union. Following five years in Hull and a solid grounding in parish ministry, Fr Rear moved to Goldthorpe in the South Riding of Yorkshire in the Sheffield diocese. It had a long Catholic tradition with close connections to Lord Halifax, for so many years the most prominent of Anglo-Catholic laymen until his death in 1934, whose family home was at Hickleton, a few miles away. Fr Rear was to be Priest-in-Charge of the Highgate Mission.[121] His Vicar was Fr Anthony Andrews.[122] In 1973 Fr Rear was appointed to his first Incumbency as Vicar of S. Margaret,[123] Thornbury, Bradford, West Yorkshire.[124] Here he served in a multi-faith, socially mixed parish with a strong Catholic tradition. It gave him the opportunity to engage in inter-faith work and ministry and, also, to study part-time for a Master's degree in Inter-Faith Studies at Hull University.

In 1989 he did not come to Walsingham as a stranger. He had come first on pilgrimage when aged seven. On that occasion his father had been so impressed with the Shrine and with Fr Patten that the family returned the following weekend. Thereafter the family made frequent pilgrimages and, as was customary then, boarded with parishioners.

---

121 The church was a chapel of ease dedicated to S. Michael. It closed in 1983
122 Vicar of S. Michael's Ladbroke Grove, Notting Hill 1974-2016. Fr Rear stayed with him in later years when a member of the General Synod of the Church of England.
123 The dedication was later changed to S. Margaret and S. James.
124 The church where Fr Michael served was the second parish church and was used from 1912 in 1991 the church was declared unsafe and demolished. The third and present St Margaret Church is combined with the Thornbury Centre and was opened in March 1999.

They also spent holidays in Sheringham which would include outings to Walsingham and the Shrine. He recalled 15th July 1961 both seeing smoke over the village and also the acrid smell of the burning of the church. The family wept as they contemplated the church ruins. In the following years he continued to make regular pilgrimages to Walsingham and to lead them from his Bradford parish. There were also some in his parish who had worshipped at Holy Trinity, Bradford, where Fr Lingwood had been curate.

Even with this long-standing connection, Fr Rear had pangs of regret, leaving Bradford, "a sinking feeling"[125] that he would no longer be able to lead pilgrimages to the Shrine. There were also understandable hesitations about leaving an inner-city parish for the very different demographic and social norms of a Norfolk village, albeit one with a national, international and ecumenical dimension. Nonetheless, he arrived to begin this new phase of his ministry. His wife, Cathy, who taught children and young adults with special needs, did not immediately move to Walsingham. Their youngest child, David, needed to stay in Bradford as he was half-way through his GCSE studies and his mother remained with him. They joined Fr Rear on the completion of David's studies, and after Cathy had been able to take early retirement. Of their two other children, Frances was studying Electronic Engineering at Reading University, and Andrew was about to go to university. Fr Rear's anxieties soon dissipated when he found that welcoming pilgrims, celebrating Mass for them on Sundays and meeting them were a pleasure. Unable to lead pilgrimages to Walsingham, he found ample compensation leading pilgrims elsewhere, not least to Rome, a city he knew well. He was also delighted to find that both the Roman Catholic Church in the village and the National Shrine were in the care of priests of the Society of Mary (Marists). In Hull he and Cathy had lived in a flat owned by the Marist Fathers, whom he came to know well, and at Goldthorpe there had been a convent of Marist Sisters. He knew them well too as the

---

125 Fr Rear in correspondence.

convent was next door to the parish church. Living in a village initially was something of a culture shock to Fr Rear, as he anticipated, but he soon and happily adjusted; knowing people, visiting homes and making connections with village organisations as well as with church groups. He was greatly helped by Mary Lockwood, wife of a retired priest, who was connected to much of the life of the village as well as to the life of the church and was able to keep him informed about cases of illness or need, and to keep him aware of the pulse of village life.

Like his predecessor, he found John Gurney "secretly very generous

but personally abstemious."[126] He admired Mr Gurney's "paternal care for the village" not least his visits to bereaved families. Fr Rear also experienced, as had his predecessor, the differing ecclesial traditions between vicarage and the Abbey. From time to time Mr Gurney would raise profound theological questions in the tersest of formulations. Hearing the Angelus on one of his rare visits to S. Mary's for Mass he asked, "How can Mary be the Mother of God, Vicar?" Fr Rear replied in similar fashion, "Something to do with Jesus being God, Mr Gurney," that seemed to satisfy him. Fr Rear did not always provide an answer that fully satisfied Mr Gurney, a teetotaller with a preference for Matins. "Why do we have all these services with wine, Vicar?" "Something to do with Jesus giving them wine at the Last Supper, Mr Gurney." "Humph," said Mr Gurney as he walked away. One of his daughters, Jean, was married to Sir Patrick Mayhew, at the time Secretary of State for Northern Ireland. He and his wife had the use of Houghton Farm, on the Gurney Estate as a safe refuge during the period of IRA terrorist activity. On one occasion Fr Rear saw "two shady-looking characters in the grounds, checking a

---

126 Fr Rear in correspondence.

window and looking as if they were casing the joint." When he, with some trepidation but rather bravely, approached them to enquire if they were looking for someone they, fortunately, turned out to be police bodyguards checking security.

Fr Rear was alert to the eccentric characters who can be found in village life and enjoyed their quirks, charm and idiosyncrasies. Rose Howell was Mr Gurney's chauffeur and also worked on the Estate. One of her several and varied tasks was to dig up the snowdrops that grew in the Abbey grounds and pack and despatch them for sale at Covent Garden. Following a casual remark made by Fr Rear to her that he had received a delivery from the Estate, a consignment of logs and that they were very large, the next day he found Rose Howell, then in her 90s, chopping the logs and neatly stacking them. Fr Rear received the gift of a pheasant once a year from the Estate but had to decline the proffered gift of pheasants from Rose Howell which, as they were interfering with her work, she had hit with her spade, as that was technically poaching. Beyond those duties, she rang the church bell at S. Giles' Houghton. She was regarded with great affection by her employers and in the village. She was still working at 90 and Mr and Mrs Gurney gave her a birthday party in the Parish Hall, attended by the whole family and most of the villagers.

Among the most devout parishioners was Miss Hatton who continued to drive despite advanced age and living in a house on the bend in the road on Knight Street which meant that she could not see oncoming traffic from either direction as she reversed into the road. Her solution was to say, the "Hail Mary" and then back out onto the road. She never had an accident. Despite the grace of Holy Orders, Canon John Brewer[127] had a less pristine driving record. Failing eyesight did not deter him for he took another retired priest with him, Fr Nixon, who could not drive but could see better than Fr Brewer, until once when Fr Nixon was distracted and Fr Brewer crashed into a parked car. Fr Brewer's final car journey was into his bathroom having

---

127 Sometime Archdeacon of Accra: Vicar, All Saints' Notting Hill.

pressed the accelerator instead of the brake. Failing hearing also added a degree of terror and embarrassment to those penitents who made their confession to him in the Shrine, when it had the potential to turn into a public event.

Another parishioner provided the opportunity for one of Fr Rear's significant contributions to the parish and village. Walter York-Easter, when employed by Bentley cars, had re-designed the winged-B mascot carried on all their cars. On his death, his widow, Dollar, wanted the mascot to be engraved on his headstone. As this offended diocesan bureaucratic sensibilities, she had a drawing produced that made the mascot look like an angel. It was duly approved. When she decided that she should sell her home, the Old Vicarage, Fr Rear wondered whether Baroness (Sue) Ryder[128] would be interested in buying it and converting it into a residential home. Fr Rear had experience of a Sue Ryder Home in Hickleton when he was curate of Goldthorpe and knew the valuable social care they provided in the community. Sue Ryder was a devout Roman Catholic and a frequent visitor to Walsingham. She had opened a Retreat House to provide a Catholic Marian centre in the village and accommodation for pilgrims. Lady Ryder and Mrs York-Easter were slightly acquainted and with Jane Nicholson, Chair of the Sue Ryder Foundation, agreed the idea suggested by Fr Rear. Mrs York-Easter gave her house to the Foundation and was provided with a flat in the house for her lifetime. The Sue Ryder Home was opened by the Duchess of Gloucester. There was residential accommodation, a nursing home and a wing for those suffering from dementia, and a Chapel where there was a Catholic and an Anglican Mass each week, and a shared Tabernacle. It cared for many local people, including Sisters of the Society of St Margaret, as well as Alan Clark, the retired Bishop of East Anglia. Lady Ryder died in 2000. The Home continued

---

128 Margaret Susan Cheshire (née Ryder), Baroness Ryder of Warsaw, Lady Cheshire, had been a member of Special Operations Executive during World War II. She founded residential homes for seriously disabled Allied soldiers. He husband, Leonard Cheshire VC., OM., DSO (later Baron Cheshire) was a RAF pilot during the War and, like his wife, a philanthropist.

under Jane Nicholson's chairmanship of the Sue Ryder Foundation. However, to much anger, distress and dismay in the village, "when she resigned in 2003 to devote herself to her new charity, FARA[129], supporting orphanages in Romania, the other trustees, who did not share the same Christian outlook, lost no time in closing down not only the Retreat House but also the Home, which was a huge loss to the village, and a great sadness that Mrs York-Easter's gift to the village people had been taken from them."[130]

In common with all parish priests. Fr Rear's life was a round of liturgical celebrations, pastoral encounters, social visiting, visiting the sick, births, marriages and deaths, meetings, committees, groups, confirmation classes, Lent courses, and, in this parish, responsibility for the Assumptiontide Lectures.[131] Walsingham offered also co-operation with the work of the Shrine, and a heightened awareness of ecumenical relations. He thought that evangelism should have a high priority. It had been many years since there had been a Parish Mission. In conjunction with Sister Anne SSM, he organised one, forming  house groups, a home visiting team, sustained by missionary services. He extended this activity to encompass the young people in the village by arranging a week in the ecumenical community of Taizé. Despite an unfortunate incident when some of the young were enticed into drink by someone who had been banned by the Taizé Brothers for

---

129 Free in Romanian.
130 Fr Rear and Jane Nicholson in correspondence.
131 As Fr Rear did not arrive in Walsingham until August 1989, he gave the Lecture himself. Subsequent lecturers, at his invitation, were Fr Vincent Blehl SJ, Revd Dr Gordon Wakefield, (the Methodist academic), Dr Eamon Duffy, Dr Nigel Yates, (both of whom Fr Rear had known when a curate in Hull where they were undergraduates at the University), Dr Julian Litten, Fr Philip Steer (the Orthodox priest in Walsingham).

past unruly behaviour, the group fully engaged with community activity, worship, Bible studies, discussion groups, informal, friendly encounters with young people from around the world.

Whereas much of a parish priest's life is one of routine and regularity, it is invariably punctured by the unexpected and contingent. Fr Rear's Sunday routine was to celebrate Mass at 9 a.m. in S. Peter's, drive through the village, to see who was in the High Street, what was on the news placard outside the newsagent, say Mass in Houghton at 10 a.m., return to S. Mary's for the 11 a.m. Mass. On only one occasion he varied that routine. He left S. Peter's after Mass, turned left rather than right, and drove through the ford, along Scarborough Road to Sunk Road. Near the Old Vicarage, he came upon a couple, Tommy and Sylvia Seaman, both Methodists. She had fallen from her bicycle, was unconscious, bleeding. Her husband was paralysed with shock. From a nearby cottage Fr Rear telephoned for an ambulance, secured a retired priest to cover at Houghton, anointed Sylvia, prayed and waited for the ambulance. Although she suffered brain damage and memory loss, she recovered sufficiently to return to work. Fr Rear had never taken that route before and never took it again.

The effects from the Second Vatican Council meant that Walsingham became an important focus for the development of ecumenical relations and co-operation. There was an Ecumenical Prayer Group which met in the Chapel of the Sue Ryder Retreat House, joint Lent courses and joint worship during the Week of Prayer for Christian Unity. Each religious community arranged its own fundraising activities, which were supported by the other churches. When Fr Peter Walters, the Shrine Priest, founded a charity 'Let the Children Live! for work among street-children in Colombia, an ecumenical committee organised fundraising events and opened a shop, its profits going to the charity. Both Fr Rear and the Roman Catholic Deacon John Hawkes participated in regular preaching on the Methodist Circuit. Fr Rear's love for dignified liturgy and ritual was also accompanied by an appreciation of the value of informal, charismatic worship. In that spirit, he began a monthly 'Songs of Praise' at S. Peter's, sometimes led by priests or ministers from other denominations.

These examples of ecumenical co-operation had come in the wake of the significant statement from ARCIC I in 1981 on Authority in the Church, at the end of the first phase of the ecumenical dialogue, and the continuing work of ARCIC II from 1983 with consideration of the doctrines of Salvation, Communion, the Teaching Authority, and the role of Mary, Mother of God. The ARCIC Final Report acknowledged that "in the past, Roman Catholic teaching that the Bishop of Rome is universal primate by divine right or law has been regarded by Anglicans as unacceptable. However, we believe that the primacy of the Bishop of Rome can be affirmed as part of God's design for the universal koinonia in terms which are compatible with both our traditions. Given such a consensus, the language of divine rights used by the First Vatican Council need no longer be seen as a matter of disagreement between us."

Hopes for reconciliation were high, at least within Anglo-Catholicism. Dr John Moorman, the Bishop of Ripon, the principal Anglican Observer to Vatican II, wrote in his Foreword to Fr Rear's first book,[132] "that doctrinally there are no substantial barriers between Rome and Canterbury and that 'One Step More' could bring about the reunion for which we all so hope." Much of ecumenical history, however, has seen a different trajectory. Although there is undoubtedly much more sustained co-operation and making common cause on many occasions, some barriers remain, and new ones have been erected.

When Fr Rear became Vicar of Walsingham, there was still an atmosphere of hope that there "was not an area whereby remaining differences of theological interpretations … can justify … continuing separation."[133] Fr Rear and Fr John Weaver, the Roman Catholic Parish Priest began a custom to join on Palm Sunday for the Blessing of Palms

---

132 One Step More between Rome and Canterbury, 1982.
133 ARCIC II: Salvation and the Church 1987.

before separating to celebrate Mass in their own churches, signifying what could be accomplished together and what remained that divided the two communions. Fr Rear made a wide contribution beyond the parish and was appointed by the Archbishop of Canterbury, George Carey, to the English Anglican-Roman Catholic Committee which shadowed the work of the International Commission.

On one occasion Fr Rear's sense of humour caused a blip in ecumenical relations. He wrote an unattributed spoof article in the Parish Magazine suggesting that new research indicated that the word "Slipper" in Slipper Chapel "came from an old English word meaning 'sleep' and that it was so named because inebriated medieval pilgrims would spend the night there to 'sleep' it off." The Roman Catholic Deacon John Hawkes reacted badly and regarded it as an attack on the Catholic Church. Fr Rear, as Editor, took full responsibility and apologised for any offence caused but, also, as Editor, could not reveal his source.

Although these local ecumenical advances continued, and although the life of the church and the village went on much the same, there were storm clouds lowering on the horizon. The movement for the ordination of women to the priesthood in the Church of England was no longer an issue on the fringe of the Church but had been garnering increasing support and incremental momentum, not least from the example of the Episcopal Church in the USA.

Following the "democratisation" of the Church of England and the inauguration of the General Synod, there was a quasi-parliamentary forum where the question was debated with some degree of regularity. Over several years, proposals for the ordination of women were supported by two-thirds majorities in the House of Bishops and the House of Clergy but failed to attain the necessary two-thirds majority in the House of Laity. Some Anglo-Catholics had accepted the ordination of women to the diaconate in the deluded expectation that it would satisfy the proponents of women's ordination. There was some justification in that the diaconate was a distinct and discrete

Holy Order that did not necessarily lead to priesthood. It turned out that it was seen not as a solution but as a condescending sop; that the question was not necessarily theological, although cast in those terms, but political, about equality, human rights, discrimination; that in the Church of England the diaconate was seen as the year of work experience, of practical training before ordination to the priesthood. The Church of England had no distinctive permanent diaconate. Nor had the Synod taken advice from distinguished theologians that the Church should have addressed the question whether or not women could be bishops, from which all else would flow. As it was, each stage was hotly contested causing increasing resentment and schism at each victory or defeat.

Fr Rear, as Rural Dean, and one of his Churchwardens, Major Patrick King, as a member of the House of Laity of General Synod, spoke at many meetings in the area and diocese as proposals came again before General Synod. He also preached about the issue and its theological implications. On one occasion at Houghton, Mr Gurney, a strong supporter of the ordination of women, walked out in the middle of the sermon. He returned at its conclusion for his wife to say in a loud voice, "You should not have walked out, John: you missed a jolly good sermon." In common with most Anglo-Catholics, Fr Rear and Major King shared the view that ecumenical developments and the ultimate prospect of reconciliation with Rome, a cause much encouraged by the visit of Pope John Paul II to Great Britain and his welcome by Archbishop Runcie, meant that the Church of England would not do anything that would undermine nor jeopardise that progress and ultimate goal. There was a widespread, although not universal, belief, among Anglo-Catholics that the proposed Measure would fail to obtain the necessary majority, albeit narrowly, in the House of Laity. Their optimism proved to be misplaced by one vote. Given that anticipation and the narrow majority, the result came as a hammer-blow. The dismay was further exacerbated when the lack of planning by Anglo-Catholics for such an outcome was exposed.

Fr Rear and Cathy knew immediately that the decision meant the end of their happy years in Walsingham. With Fr Roy Fellows, the Administrator of the Shrine and the Shrine Priest, Fr Peter Walters, Fr Rear realised the decision marked the end of their priestly ministry in the Church of England and, as a married man, it seemed to Fr Rear the prospect of the end of his priesthood altogether. Whatever the future held, Fr Rear recognised that "what I had all my life believed about the Church of England, that it was part or a branch of the Catholic Church, as the Oxford Movement had taught, turned out not to be true."[134] Together with other priests in the Norwich Diocese, he went to see Bishop Alan Clark of East Anglia. He had been Co-Chairman of ARCIC and, unlike some of his episcopal brethren, had a keen understanding of Anglo-Catholicism and, like Cardinal Hume, was not unsympathetic.

For Fr Rear, as for many parish priests in the aftermath of the vote, whatever their personal circumstances or decisions, they had a responsibility to their parishioners. There were, in effect, three groups: those who determined to leave the Church of England, for Rome or the Orthodox; those who would remain and accept the Church of England's decision to ordain women, some reluctantly, others enthusiastically; those who would remain within the Church of England with provision to be made to enable them to do so in good conscience. There was to be two years of uncertainty before the first ordinations of women would take place. Division and departures were inevitable but it was Fr Rear's intention that individual consciences should be respected; that there should be no recrimination.

To provide a framework for the process of discussion and decision, Fr Rear related his experience when visiting his daughter, Frances, in Kenya, where she had spent three years with VSO[135] teaching in a remote school. S. Mary's parishioners had raised £2,000 for the installation of solar power in the school. There he had met a Community of Roman

---

134 Fr Rear in correspondence.
135 Voluntary Service Overseas.

Catholic Sisters who surprised him by explaining that the founder of their Order had been an Anglican priest, John Mason Neale. He had founded the Sisters of S. Margaret with whom Fr Rear worked in Walsingham. He had founded the Society of S. Margaret in 1855 but in 1868 the then Reverend Mother had decided to become a Roman Catholic. When, having been advised by Cardinal Manning to do so, she told her community, all but one Sister and one Novice followed her. Those who converted flourished and subsequently helped to evangelise much of Kenya and Uganda. The two nuns who did not convert were housed at Haggerston and also prospered in their work, moving to East Grinstead, and establishing the daughter house in Walsingham, as well as in other parts of the world. Fr Rear used this illustration to establish the principle of following individual conscience in the discussions that needed to occur and the decisions that each individual had to make, so that all could flourish and each find blessing.

For those who wished to remain in the Church of England with appropriate provision, *Forward in Faith* was founded as an umbrella organisation for Anglo-Catholics. A solution was found and provision was enacted in the parliamentary legislation that permitted the ordination of women to the priesthood, to enable PCCs to pass either Resolution A or B, or both.[136] A further provision was made in an Act of Synod, commonly called Resolution C, which enabled PCCs who had passed either of the Resolutions to petition the diocesan bishop to provide alternative episcopal oversight by Provincial Episcopal Visitors.[137] During the PCC discussions in 1993, as provisions became

---

136 Resolution A: That this PCC would not accept a woman as the minister who presides at the celebration of Holy Communion or pronounces the Absolution in the parish. Resolution B: That this PCC would not accept a woman as the incumbent or priest in charge of the benefice or as a team vicar. These Resolutions were repealed by the Bishops and Priests (Consecration and Ordination of Women) Measure 2014. Other arrangements were put in place.

137 Bishops of Ebbsfleet and Richborough in the Province of Canterbury. Bishop

clear, Fr Rear pointed out the impossibility of a priest bringing people into a church whose teachings he could not accept.[138] Fr Rear's eirenic approach, respecting individual conscience continued to underpin discussion. It was noted that the "meeting ended on a note of sadness, but with members determined that charity should prevail."[139] At a subsequent meeting, Fr Rear remained opposed to the Measure and anticipated that some 30 members of the congregation might submit to the authority of the Roman Catholic Church[140] but he emphasised that he remained parish priest for all equally regardless of their opinions over "this divisive, tragic issue."[141] Fr Rear did not attend the PCC Meeting where the Resolutions were adopted, as he had then decided to resign. Conscious that Walsingham had become a focal point, nationally as well as locally and as an example of solidarity the PCC adopted Resolution A, 16 For 3 Against 0 Abstentions, and Resolution B, 17 For 1 Against 1 Abstention.[142]

The parting of friends is always painful, particularly when conscience and religious susceptibilities are involved. John Henry Newman's conversion in 1845 had set a precedent. Fr Rear felt that "the parting was characterised by understanding [it was] sad but for most people not acrimonious."[143] After celebrating his last Mass as Vicar, at the parish AGM a presentation was made and kind sentiments were expressed. Fr Rear and his family were able to continue to live in

---

of Beverley in the Province of York. The Bishop of Maidstone provides oversight for Evangelical parishes that do not accept women's ordination. The Bishop of Fulham provides oversight for parishes in the dioceses of London and Southwark. There is one diocesan bishop who does not ordain women and two suffragan bishops.

138 PCC Minutes 28 June 1993.
139 PCC Minutes 28 June 1993.
140 32 people left AGM Minutes 1995.
141 PCC Minutes 20 September 1993.
142 PCC Minutes 10 January 1994. For a legal technicality the vote was taken again at the beginning of the Interregnum: Resolution A 17 For 0 Against 0 Abstentions: Resolution B 16 For 1 Against 0 Abstentions.
143 Fr Rear in correspondence.

the vicarage until new accommodation was found. A generous local farmer, David Allingham and his wife, Annie, provided a cottage in Syderstone. Given the substantial number of Anglo-Catholic priests who converted to Rome, Pope John Paul II instituted a system which devolved authority to local bishops to deal with applications, which were then submitted to Rome with recommendations. Having followed a period of instruction and study Fr Rear was ordained.

Walsingham had not seen the last of Fr Rear, nor Fr Rear of Walsingham. Once Fr Rear had been ordained, the new Bishop of East Anglia, Peter Smith, suggested to Fr Alan Williams SM, the Director of the National Shrine, that Fr Rear should minister there. After some hesitation and having consulted Fr Peter Cobb, the Master of the Guardians of the Shrine, about whether or not this would be appropriate or politic, who gave a positive response, Fr Rear began his new work. Based at the National Shrine during the week, he celebrated Sunday Mass at Dersingham. After a year, Fr Peter Allen SM, the Parish Priest, became ill and, as the Marist Fathers had no-one then available to replace him, Fr Rear was asked by Bishop Peter and Fr Williams to become the Parish Administrator. There were obvious sensitivities to be considered and Bishop Peter discussed the unique appointment with the Bishop of Norwich.

Fr Rear and Cathy did not live in the village and he took care in all his work and contacts to avoid trespassing denominational boundaries. He and Fr Keith Haydon established a good relationship, jointly leading a pilgrimage of Anglicans and Roman Catholics to Rome, celebrating Mass on alternate days which all attended but without inter-communion, movingly marking where they agreed and where they remained separated. He participated in the Week of Prayer for Christian Unity and the Lent courses, and at Funeral Masses, with the permission of the Bishop of East Anglia, he agreed with Fr Haydon that they would take the Holy Sacrament to each other's churches to communicate the faithful.

He served in Walsingham for three years. When a new Parish Priest was appointed, Fr Rear became the Parish Priest in Fakenham where he served the rest of his ministry. He and Cathy retired to Manningtree where he assisted in the local parish and became Chaplain to the University of Suffolk. Fr Rear greatly appreciated "the extraordinary generosity and friendship" that the parishioners of Walsingham had extended to him since his conversion and he returned in 2018 to preach in S. Mary's on the 60th anniversary of Fr Patten's death and in 2019 gave an address in the Shrine on S. John Henry Newman. He also wrote two more books, one on the history and meaning of Walsingham, and the other, a Pilgrim's Guide to Rome. And in 2020 he and Cathy returned once more to the place where he had lived and served, and loved, Walsingham. They were greatly moved that one of their first visitors was Fr Harri Williams, the Parish Priest, who came with a bottle of wine, a plant for Cathy and a card in which he had written, "Welcome Home."

KEITH FRANK MICHAEL HAYDON

Fr Keith Frank Michael Haydon was instituted and licensed as Parish Priest on 5th May 1995.[144] With a sad inevitability, following the General Synod decision to permit the ordination of women to the priesthood, the Church of England, particularly its Anglo-Catholic members, had entered a period of acute tension and debilitating uncertainty. Walsingham was a microcosm of the tribulations faced by the Catholic wing of the Church of England. Although not a majority, there had been a significant number of parishioners who had converted to Roman Catholicism and Fr Haydon inherited a depleted congregation and a degree of demoralisation. Mass attendance naturally had been affected by the exodus of worshippers, among them several who had held significant posts in parish administration and were prominent in its life. Although both Walsingham and Barsham PCCs had clearly stated that they did not wish to appoint a woman priest to the vacancy, neither body pursued Alternative Episcopal Oversight. This led to some anxiety among pilgrims. Some priests on pilgrimage were uncertain about concelebrating the Pilgrimage Mass on Sunday morning in S. Mary's in case they found themselves in the company of those of heterodox views. These hesitations were overcome by a recognition and acceptance that the views and orders of the principal celebrant provided sufficient theological protection for all but the most tender of consciences.

Fr Haydon was also aware that in the aftermath of the Synod

---

144 By an Order in Council 18th October 1995: The Benefice was now that of S. Mary and All Saints, Little Walsingham, with S. Peter and Houghton S. Giles, and the Benefice of East Barsham with North Barsham and West Barsham, to be known as the Benefice of Walsingham, Houghton and Barsham. The parish of East Barsham, the parish of North Barsham and the parish of West Barsham shall also be united to create a new parish which shall be named the Parish of East, North and West Barsham.

decision ecumenical relations in Walsingham were, to a degree, strained. Those who had left S. Mary's had not moved far away, only a few hundred yards, to the Catholic Church. There they had assimilated swiftly, not least as altar servers, readers and Eucharistic Ministers, playing leading parts, as they had done as Anglicans. Although, given the trauma of separation, mutual respect and harmony, and cordial relationships were restored, even improved upon, Fr Haydon, in his early days, felt that "there were occasions where [he] thought [he] had landed in Belfast or the Liverpool of old – and while there were no hand-painted slogans or banners to be seen around the village … it was not unusual to hear cries of 'traitor' or 'Judas' echoing across the High Street as former congregants passed each other."[145]

To face these problems Walsingham had in its new Incumbent a priest steeped in the Anglo-Catholic tradition: a cradle Anglo-Catholic, a scion of East End London Anglo-Catholicism. His maternal grandmother had been brought up as a strict Baptist but, as a result of a mission led by Fr Stanton,[146] at the turn of the 20th century she had been converted to the Church of England and was, for the rest of her life, a staunch, devout Anglo-Catholic. She had a great veneration for the Blessed Virgin Mary, and sang Marian hymns while doing her chores. She and her daughter, Kathleen, Fr Haydon's mother, lived in Stoke Newington and attended the Mission Church of S. Paul, a daughter church of West Hackney Parish Church. S. Paul's Church was at the bottom of their garden and was one of the London churches that was entirely Roman in its liturgy, ceremonial and teaching. Reputedly, it only betrayed its Church of England identity with copies of *Hymns Ancient and Modern* shelved near the main door. When S. Paul's Mission Church closed in the 1930s,[147] his mother and grandmother attended the Parish Church. His mother held the

---

145 Fr Haydon in correspondence.
146 Fr Arthur Henry Stanton (1839-1913). Curate S. Alban the Martyr, Holborn (1862-1913).
147 It became a garage but a large crucifix and a plaque bearing the names of those from the locality who had lost their lives in the Great War, remained

responsible position of Sunday School Superintendent. The church had been solidly Anglo-Catholic since the 1860s. Fr Mackonochie,[148] who as the Vicar of S. Alban's Holborn had Fr Stanton as his curate, had led a Mission in the early 1880s. As a result of that Mission the other side of Fr Haydon's forebears, his paternal grandparents, as youngsters, were brought into the Church. There was a further connection with S. Alban's as Fr Haydon's mother was a flower-girl there for the Feast of Corpus Christi on several occasions. At one stage of her early life Kathleen had been keen to join the Sisters of Bethany as a postulant but the Reverend Mother had dissuaded her, saying that she was insufficiently "robust" for the rigours of the Religious Life. That Kathleen later became a member of the Land Army and was active in Civil Defence during World War II, and gave birth to three sons, all of whom grew to over six foot in height, perhaps proves that nuns are not always right.[149] His mother also had a further Anglo-Catholic connection. She became a dressmaker in the West End of London and often attended the early daily Mass at All Saints' Margaret Street.

Fr Haydon's father, Frank, had been a regular soldier in the King's Royal Rifle from 1931 to 1945. He served mainly in India until 1939 when he returned to England on the outbreak of War. In 1940 he served at Dunkirk. He was not among those rescued by the flotilla of small craft. Rather, he was captured and marched to a Prisoner of War Camp in Poland, where he remained for the rest of the War, only to be released in 1945. He was permanently scarred by his experiences, was angry with God and was absent from faith for many years. Fr Haydon

---

in place on the wall for many years until the building was demolished in the early 1970s.

148 Fr Alexander Heriot Mackonochie (1825-1887). Perpetual Curate S. Alban the Martyr, Holborn (1862-1882) Vicar. S. Peter, London Docks (1882-1883). Returned to live in the Clergy House and assist at S. Alban's, Holborn until his death.

149 Fr Haydon, in correspondence, harbours suspicions that his mother was not "posh" enough for Reverend Mother. Of course, had she joined the Order Fr Haydon and his two brothers would not have been born.

was born to Kathleen and Frank in 1946. His parents were living at the time in Haggerston Road, Hackney, a short distance from S. Saviour's Convent of the Sisters of S. Margaret. He was born and was brought up in an all-embracing Anglo-Catholic family and community.

On Sundays he attended early Mass with his grandmother and Sunday School, which was run by his Godmother, in the afternoon. The Parish Church had been destroyed by bombing in 1940 but the congregation met in a former school building in which one section was made into a chapel, furnished with what had been salvaged from other bombed churches in the area. The parish was merged with S. Barnabas, Shackwell Row, Dalston, under its Incumbent, Fr John Eastaugh.[150] He had been trained at the College of the Resurrection, Mirfield, as had most of his curates. He was also assisted by Licensed Parish Workers and, from the Church Army but with Anglo-Catholic leanings, Sister Beeton. She ran the Wolf Pack whose meetings began with the *Angelus*. It was a typical Anglo-Catholic parish of its time and place. The principal service was the Parish Mass followed by breakfast, Mass was said daily. There were numerous groups, guilds, societies, fraternities and confraternities: Cubs, Scouts, Guides, Mothers' Union, Church of England Men's Society among them. From the age of six Fr Haydon served as a Boat Boy, even up at 6 a.m. for Mass on festal days. From the age of eight, he served at weekday Masses; from the age of 11 he served the Saturday Mass for the Wantage Sisters at their house in Stamford Hill. Thoughts about becoming a priest began between the ages of eight or nine. He was caught up in the ritual and the comprehensive life of the parish and community and, impressionable as a young boy, he saw the priests whom he knew as "lively characters" and he "wanted to be like them."[151] He spoke to them about these early intimations of a vocation and, while they were both sympathetic and encouraging, they told him of the need for university education, which for an East End boy, at the time, seemed another world.

---

150 The Rt Revd John Eastaugh (1920-1990) Bishop of Hereford 1974-1990.
151 Fr Haydon in correspondence.

At primary school he missed sitting the 11+ Examination having been taken to hospital on the day of the examination suffering from appendicitis. Consequently, he attended Hackney Free and Parochial School. It was a markedly different environment from his experience of the church. Religion in the school was "dire,"[152] only one other pupil in his first year was confirmed with him. He excelled at cricket and football, representing the School in both. He enjoyed music, learning the violin and recorder, he acted in school plays but academic achievement eluded him. A sense of vocation persisted, however, but the path to its attainment remained elusive. After completing his secondary education, he found employment as a Junior Clerk at Hackney Hospital, which provided him with a good grounding in efficient administration. Still, he felt the call to ordination, yet continued to recognise that the absence of academic qualifications would be a barrier but one that might be overcome by obtaining appropriate lay experience as an alternative route. With the encouragement of his Vicar, Fr Preston,[153] he spent two years working in a children's home for boys who had special physical and education needs. Northorpe Hall was situated near Mirfield. As well as undertaking his duties at the Hall, from bricklaying to visiting problem families in Leeds, he was able to spend time in the Community of the Resurrection, mixing with monks and ordinands, especially for one memorable Holy Week.

He returned to London to work with the Church Army at a hostel in Stepney. There he encountered the realities of homelessness, not only realising how easy it was to lose house and home but also its attendant problems of drink and drugs. He also discovered nearby S. Mary, Cable Street and Fr Peter Clynick SSC its parish priest[154]. Both the liturgy (Fr Haydon attended the 7 a.m. Mass daily, work

---

152 Fr Haydon in correspondence.
153 The Revd Preb. Frederick Arnold Preston MBE Rector, Hackney West, S. Barnabas with S. Paul. He died in 2001.
154 The Revd Peter Clynick (1917-1985) Priest in Charge S. Mary, Cable Street 1958-1968, Vicar 1968-1985.

timetable permitting) and the social life of the parish were much more conducive and sustaining than the rather "austere and fanatical evangelicalism" he found at the Church Army Hostel.[155]

The new Bishop of Stepney, Trevor Huddleston CR[156], had returned from Africa. For his work there, over many years, he was a hero to many, including Fr Haydon, for his support of the Anti-Apartheid movement in South Africa. Fr Haydon had attended, with his mother and a contingent from their parish, a rally at the Royal Albert Hall. As Bishop of Stepney, Fr Huddleston lived near the hostel where Fr Haydon worked and, even more fortunately, he often said the early Mass on Thursday, which Fr Haydon attended. Although rather in awe of him, Fr Haydon spoke to Bishop Huddleston about his sense of vocation, while acknowledging his background and lack of a degree. Over tea, the Bishop said that he thought that Fr Haydon had a call to ordination that ought to be tested. He sponsored him to attend a Selection Conference and suggested that suitable training would be available at Brasted Place College in Kent. For many years Brasted specialised in preparing candidates for ordination training at theological colleges who had missed higher, and sometimes secondary, education. Its students had followed diverse secular careers; in the Armed Forces, as policemen, clerks, car mechanics, shop workers, all sorts and conditions of men.

Recommended for training, with the support of his Bishop, he gained a place at Brasted and received a solid grounding in Church History, Biblical Studies, Greek and Hebrew, towards a qualification in the General Ordination Examination. He took up the offer of a place at Cuddesdon Theological College, where he thought of himself as "the first peasant" to attend the "country club for gentlemen which

---

155 Fr Haydon in correspondence.
156 The Most Revd Ernest Urban Trevor Huddleston CR,. KCMG (1913-1998) In South Africa 1943-1956, Bishop of Masasi 1960-1968, Bishop of Stepney 1968-1978, Bishop of Mauritius and Archbishop of the Indian Ocean 1978-1983.

produced bishops."[157] He was ordained to the diaconate in 1975 by Bishop Huddleston to serve his title in north east London at S. Peter's, Beauvoir Town. His mother had lived to see him selected for training but, much to his sorrow, had died before he was ordained. At S. Peter's his training Incumbent was Fr John Baggley, who had trained at Kelham. It was a multi-cultural, ethnically mixed parish, increasingly socially diverse as the area became gentrified. It proved a happy mix. He also assisted in the chaplaincy of the local hospital, where he had worked as a porter during college vacations. Given how firmly rooted he was in Anglo-Catholicism, it seemed entirely appropriate that his first sick communicant was an elderly lady who had been confirmed by the saintly Bishop Edward King of Lincoln.

Fr Haydon was ordained priest in 1976 and offered Mass for the first time on S. Peter's Day. His first Mass of Our Lady was celebrated in S. Saviour's Priory[158]. Years later some of the Sisters there transferred to Walsingham. He said Mass regularly for the Sisters and also did some painting and decorating for them in the redundant vicarage in which they lived while the Priory was re-built.

His first curacy was cut short when he became seriously ill with Ulcerative Colitis, a disease of the large intestine.[159] It was suggested that work in a country parish might be less strenuous. Consequently, in 1977, he moved to Somerset as Curate of S. Thomas' Wells. His Incumbent was Fr Ross Thompson.[160] He was in the process of transforming a low, dull, pedestrian parish into an Anglo-Catholic one; "from Mink and Matins to Bingo and Benediction."[161] Work in

---

157 Fr Haydon in correspondence.
158 During Mass, after reciting the first part of the Canon, he turned two pages by mistake and went into the Paternoster. The nuns were too polite to point out the error but, as he later learned, some thought that he had wanted to avoid praying for the Pope.
159 Bishop Huddleston visited him in hospital, between flights at Heathrow. Other patients commented that none of their bosses had been to visit them.
160 Later General Secretary of the Church Union. He later converted to Roman Catholicism.
161 Fr Haydon in correspondence.

a busy parish was combined with a part-time chaplaincy at the local psychiatric hospital, which brought its several challenges of pastoral care and conducting worship amidst disruptions and shouting, from which care staff absented themselves for a smoke. This might not quite have been the sedate ministry conducive to his recovery from his illness. Ulcerative Colitis is rarely cured, rather it has to be managed. Fr Haydon was still prescribed heavy medication and steroids. During his curacy, he joined a pilgrimage to the Shrine of Our Lady of Lourdes. He "took a full part in the pilgrimage and was able to say Mass for the many Anglicans there at the time ... Shortly after returning home, tests showed that the condition had cleared up." He threw away his tablets.[162]

After recovery and three fulfilling years in Wells, Fr Haydon moved to his first incumbency as Team Vicar in Weston-super-Mare. He was in charge of S. Saviour's church, a "moderately high parish" as was indicated by his predecessor as Vicar being always addressed by his title or as Mister. He resided in retirement, after a long ministry at S. Saviour's, only a short distance beyond the parish boundary. This is not usually an easy circumstance for the new Incumbent and Fr Haydon was regularly told by parishioners that they had been talking to the Vicar. However, despite those annoyances, Fr Haydon found its congregation sympathetic to change. In his first year, Fr Haydon introduced a daily Mass, brought the liturgy into line with contemporary practice, and installed a nave altar. He also had support and assistance from a retired Parish Worker, Edna Guthrie, a kindred spirit, who had worked in the East End of London and had prepared Reggie and Ronnie Kray for confirmation.[163] Initially a predominantly elderly congregation, its numbers grew considerably

---

162 The Catholic Herald carried the dramatic headline, "Dying Anglican Priest in mercy dash to Lourdes".
163 Ronald Kray (1933-1995), Reginald Kray (1933-2000) Both sentenced to life imprisonment for murder in 1969. On their joint headstone are the words: Grant them eternal rest, O Lord and let light perpetual shine upon them." Edna Guthrie instructed them well, in this at least. She also prepared

and young families joined and there was much support from many members of the parish. Money was raised for the building a new hall next to the church.

In 1984 an opportunity arose for Fr Haydon to re-establish his working relationship with Fr Ross Thompson. Fr Thompson had become Team Rector of Cowley in east Oxford and Fr Haydon joined him as Team Vicar. He was familiar with the area from his time at Cuddesdon and had enjoyed a parish placement there. Cowley was then a large working class parish served by three churches. The major employer was the Cowley Assembly Plant, formerly the factory of Morris Motors. There were some 40,000 employees. From the East End of London to east Oxford may have been a return to familiar urban territory. The parish had benefited from a succession of effective parish priests and the work of the Society of S. John the Evangelist (the Cowley Fathers). There were good schools, much goodwill and healthy congregations.

As Fr Haydon's first sick communicant in the East End had been confirmed by Bishop King, his first sick communicant in east Oxford was an elderly man who, as a small boy, had served at the last Mass celebrated by Fr Richard Meux Benson, the founder of SSJE[164], before age and fragility confined him to bed. Fr Haydon served for three years as Team Vicar, followed by eight years as Team Rector. The organisation and day by day activity of the parish was not much altered from earlier years. There was a Team of four priests, a Church Army Sister and, for some years, a community of nuns from Wantage.[165] Fr Haydon also served as Local Vicar for priests who were

---

Fr Haydon's sons for Confirmation. "They have been dining out on this ever since. To date they have kept out of jail." Fr Haydon in correspondence.

164 Fr Richard Meux Benson (1829-1915) He founded the Mission Priests of S. John the Evangelist, with two others, in 1865. It was the first Religious Order for men founded in the Church of England since the Reformation.

165 The Community of S. Mary the Virgin, Wantage, founded in 1843 by the Vicar of Wantage, Fr William John Butler.

members of the Society of the Holy Cross (SSC)[166]. He said Mass at Fairacres Convent for the Community of the Sisters of the Love of God, also for those at the Convent of the All Saints Sisters of the Poor. There were links with S. Stephen's House for parish placements and preaching practice.[167] One of the ordinands who met Fr Haydon at S. Stephen's House remembered that first meeting at which Fr Haydon produced a purple stole from his inside jacket pocket and said, "just in case I am stopped in the street." That image of a priest "fully equipped to administer the sacramental love of God wherever and whenever required" stayed with that ordinand until today.[168] Fr Haydon chaired, at various times, the Boards of Governors of three Primary Schools in the parish. He and the parish weathered the storm of the ordination of women and he became a founding member of *Forward in Faith*.

Fr Haydon came to Walsingham following a chance meeting with Major Patrick King at a *Forward in Faith* rally in 1994 and was told that no one had been found to replace Fr Rear. After much thought, Fr Haydon wrote to the Bishop of Norwich[169] who had been Bishop of Taunton when Fr Haydon was in the Diocese of Bath and Wells. Following the meeting and later meeting the Bishop of Lynn,[170] he was recommended to the Patrons and the Parish Representatives and secured the appointment.

Like most Anglo-Catholics, he knew Walsingham. He had first visited in 1956, aged 10, for a three day pilgrimage. He stayed in the Hospice, took his meals in the Pilgrims' Hall and recalled the clergy

---

166 Societas Sanctae Crucis

167 I was present on one occasion when a member of the group of which I was a member preached in S. James' Cowley.

168 Fr Robert Coates SSC now Vicar of S. Augustine, Bexhill-on-Sea in correspondence.

169 The Rt Revd Peter Nott (1933-2018) Bishop of Taunton 1977-1985, Bishop of Norwich 1985-1999.

170 The Rt Revd David Conner KCVO Bishop of Lynn 1994-1998 Dean of Windsor since 1998.

sitting at the top table, where Fr Patten presided, and hearing "gales of laughter."[171] He next visited in 1961, the year of the celebration for the 900th anniversary of the appearance of Our Lady to the Lady Richeldis. From then he went almost every year and led pilgrimages from 1976 to 1995. On his appointment he had a feeling of "coming home" rather than a sense of moving to a new, unfamiliar parish.[172] He saw his initial task, following the damage and disunity caused by the General Synod decision, to bring some cheer, optimism and a sense of purpose to parish life and to bring the parishes in the Benefice closer together in worship[173] and communal activities. He was fortunate to have a cohort of active retired priests to ensure daily Mass at S. Mary's, to provide some weekday Masses at S. Peter's and S. Giles' in addition to Sunday celebrations, to restore Sunday Mass to East Barsham and a monthly Sunday service at North Barsham and West Barsham,

As tensions eased, church and parish life recovered its balance, routine and regularity. Weekend pilgrimages in season saw S. Mary's fill to overflowing. On his arrival by moped at S. Mary's on Sunday morning from one of his other parishes, he frequently had, happily, to struggle through a crowd to gain access to church. Whenever he was in the High Street he regularly met priests and people whom he knew from his own days as a pilgrim. The Bishop of Edmonton, Brian

---

171 Fr Haydon in correspondence.
172 Fr Haydon in correspondence.
173 He had suggested that on his first Sunday in the parish there might be a Benefice Mass. This was agreed by the PCC (13 in favour, 7 against). However, "in view of the vote, the Incumbent be asked to rethink the idea of only one joint Eucharist in S. Mary's for the whole Benefice on his first Sunday in the parish." (13 in favour, 5 against 1 abstention) PCC Minutes 8 February 1995. At the Institution service Fr Haydon announced, during the customary notices, that on the following morning he would celebrate the Eucharist for the first time in the Benefice at 9.30 am in S. Mary's. Over seventy people attended and at the last minute the Mass had to be transferred from the Guilds Chapel into the body of the church. He had his Benefice Mass.

Masters[174] and the Bishop of Richborough, Edwin Barnes[175] frequently visited. After the dark night some light and joy had been restored.[176] Even without the regular influx of pilgrims, S. Mary's, S. Peter's and S. Giles' had good sized congregations, although noticeably lacking in younger people. To help to fill the lacuna, Fr Haydon sought ways to engage that age group. He accepted an invitation to be a Governor of Walsingham Primary School (not then a Church school) and to develop links between School and Church. Not long afterwards, he chaired the Governors. He instituted a weekly after-school society, the Compass Club, alternating weekly between younger and older children. Activities included outings to diverse places of interest, and not always the most obvious, such as Wells Lifeboat Station, Titchwell Nature Reserve, but also to a doctor's surgery, after hours. There were also craft sessions, visits from representatives of public organisations, the police, RSPCA among them. Christingle services were held at S. Peter's. Another popular event involving church and school was the introduction in 1996 of the Mothering Friday service, held in S. Peter's Church. Members of the Mothers' Union went into the village school earlier in the week to help the children make cards which they gave their mothers at the Mothering Friday service.

The parish was fortunate that Janet Marshall was appointed to run the Shrine's Education Department. She and her family worshipped at S. Mary's where she volunteered to re-form the Sunday School (known as the Trekkers) for activities in the Parish Hall before coming into church for the Offertory. Young people became servers, several were confirmed and many joined the Shrine's highly successful annual Youth Pilgrimages. Children also regularly formed a Nativity Tableau during the traditional Service of Nine Lessons and Carols. In one year

---

174 The Rt Revd Brian Masters (1932-1998) Bishop of Fulham 1982-1984, Bishop of Edmonton 1984-1998.
175 The Rt Revd Edwin Barnes (1935-2019) Bishop of Richborough 1995-2001.
176 Fr Haydon's sense of humour was evident when he altered the words of the hymn *Faith of Our Fathers* from "living still, in spite of dungeon, fire and sword" to read "in spite of Synod, fire and sword".

a two-day old baby, born to an Orthodox couple, was in the manger. It is claimed that "there was not a dry eye in the place."[177]

Fr Haydon was adept at responding to historic anniversaries and momentous current events with élan and sensitivity. In 1997 for the 75th Anniversary of the installation of the image of Our Lady in S. Mary's, he orchestrated a "re-enactment" with flower girls strewing petals, the pealing of bells, a sermon from the Administrator of the Shrine, Fr Martin Warner[178] from the steps of the font, a sermon by the Abbot of Alton, and the celebrations concluding with Benediction given by the Bishop of Edmonton. All was marshalled by Fr Beaumont Brandie.[179] As an ecumenical courtesy, Fr Haydon had been persuaded that Anglican priests should bow to the Blessed Sacrament rather than genuflect. This they did  while their Roman brethren executed impeccable genuflections. In the same year a joint service was held following the death of Diana, Princess of Wales[180] when some 800 gathered in S. Mary's. Shootings in Dunblane in 1996 where 16 primary school children and one teacher were killed, and 15 injured caused widespread shock. Fr Haydon and Fr Peter Allen, the Roman Catholic Director of the National Shrine jointly held a service in a packed church, among whom were children from local schools. Another revival, suggested by the British Legion, and happily taken up by Fr Haydon, was a Ceremony of Remembrance at the War Memorial in Little Walsingham on 11th

---

177 Fr Haydon in correspondence.
178 Canon of S. Paul's Cathedral, London, 2003-2010, Bishop of Whitby 2010-2012, Bishop of Chichester from 2012.
179 The Revd Canon Beaumont Brandie MBE (1940-2020) In 1977 he was Team Rector of the Resurrection, Brighton.
180 Diana, Princess of Wales (1961-1997) was killed in a motor accident in Paris.

November each year. On the first occasion an attendance of some 80 people successfully launched the restoration of the tradition.

In addition to the regular round of parish activities, there were excursions, that were well supported. A coach party travelled to S. Paul's Cathedral for a *Forward in Faith* Mass at which Mother Teresa SSM preached. Another *Forward in Faith* Mass was celebrated at Aylesford Priory in Kent, and a parish pilgrimage was made to the Shrine of Our Lady of Egmanton in Nottinghamshire. Fr Haydon continued the tradition in the parish of imaginative fundraising and social activities. He instituted a New Year meal for the several congregations in the Benefice in the Shrine Refectory, followed by "homespun entertainment," notably several Sisters performing a sketch dressed as Telly Tubbies.[181] It was after this event that one of the three remaining original Sisters from Haggerston, Sister Julian, said to him: "It was just like when Father [Patten] was here."[182] He also opened the vicarage to host social and fund-raising events. He also entertained the retired clergy who assisted in the parishes, to thank them for their contributions which made it possible to maintain a full calendar of services and the liturgical life of the churches. At Christmas he also entertained local farmers, estate workers and local business people in the vicarage. For one year (1997) S. Mary's had a Charity Shop in the High Street, by courtesy of the Walsingham Estate, until new tenants were found. This enterprise was run by Nora Claxton and raised funds for the church and parish as well as providing a place to meet and to welcome pilgrims and visitors.

Amidst this activity, attention was also given to the maintenance of the fabric of the churches in the Benefice. At All Saints, East

---

181 A popular children's entertainment on television.
182 Fr Haydon in correspondence.

Barsham plans were drawn up and Fr Haydon initiated the work for the installation of electricity, heating and lighting in the church. Previously there had been no heating and illumination had been by candlelight. The interior of S. Giles' church was re-decorated, as was the interior of S. Peter's, where there were also repairs to the roof. S. Mary's also underwent a complete re-decoration, as well as roof repairs, the installation of a new heating system, the renovation of and improvements to the organ. In the graveyard, the wooden cross which marked Fr Patten's grave and had worn badly over the years, was replaced with a headstone. The cross was preserved inside the church. An icon of the Divine Mercy was also installed in the church.

The appointment of Fr Michael Rear to be in charge of the Roman Catholic Parish Church might have been seen as insensitive and a cause for contention. However, as Fr Haydon and Fr Rear had worked together, and knew each other fairly well, as members of the Committee of the Church Literature Association, no friction arose and they established an harmonious and constructive relationship and smooth co-operation. Fr Haydon's sister-in-law was a Marist Sister and he knew some of the Sisters who were based in Walsingham, who were kind and helpful. They also provided somewhere for Fr Haydon and Bishop Peter Smith of East Anglia to smoke after events. The Marist Fathers who ran the National Shrine and the parish were also friendly and keen to resume joint activities which had, unsurprisingly, fractured and lapsed during the interregnum. Both the National Shrine Directors during Fr Haydon's period of office, Fr Peter Allen SM and Fr Alan Williams SM,[183] delivered Assumptiontide Lectures at his invitation.[184] In reviving joint services and events, they were joined, for the first time, by the Methodist congregation in the village.

In 1996 joint Lent courses, Rosary groups and Stations of the Cross were re-established, as was the joint Palm Sunday Blessing of Palms,

---

183 Now Bishop of Brentwood.
184 The other Lecturers invited by Fr Haydon were The Revd Dr Robert Hannaford and Dean Leif Norrgärd.

followed by a procession which ended with the exchange of the Kiss of Peace before proceeding to their respective churches to complete the liturgical celebrations. Friends of Fr Peter Allen owned the ruins of the Friary and he and Fr Haydon were able to use the site for the Palm Sunday Liturgy. In the following year they were also able to use the Friary site to hold a joint Summer Fête in glorious weather that was well supported by parishioners, villagers, pilgrims and tourists.

When leading a successful ecumenical pilgrimage, jointly with Fr Rear, to Rome and Assisi, Fr Haydon preached in the church of S. Gregorio. In his sermon he saw in S. Gregory the Great a shared heritage, in that "our Christian Faith is rooted equally in the local and the universal." He emphasised "the importance of the local church needing to look beyond its own immediate confines and concerns and to link with the universal in order that the Gospel of Christ may more effectively be brought to bear upon the needs and concerns of all people" and he pointed to "the dilemma that Catholic-minded Anglicans need to address ... as we strive to come to terms with a crucial Synodical decision in 1992, when it might be said that the local became out of tune with the universal."

In the space of a few years, after a distressing, difficult and divisive time for the parish, Fr Haydon had effected not only a degree of stability[185] but had instilled a sense of purpose, mission, engagement, renewal and reconciliation. There had been numerous revivals of lapsed practice and several innovations that signalled a recovery of confidence. Sadly, however, what he had once described to a BBC interviewer as "the best job in the Church of England" came to a sudden end owing to personal circumstances and difficulties that necessitated his resignation. It was a tearful departure.

He moved back to the West Country. After a time, he was able to resume his priestly ministry in Barnstaple, assisting at the parish church and also in a local hospital. He returned to full-time ministry in 2009 as Curate at S. John the Evangelist, Sutton-on-Plym, Plymouth,

---

185 AGM Minutes 2000.

also at S. Simon, Mount Gould and S. Mary, Laira, both Mission Churches of S. John's. He was subsequently appointed Priest in Charge following the death in office of the Parish Priest, Fr Patrick Allen.[186] Fr Haydon retired in 2016 but for two years he served at S. John the Evangelist, Bovey Tracey during a long interregnum. He now assists at S. Peter's and S. Francis, Plymouth.

Steeped in the Anglo-Catholic tradition, he served only a relatively brief ministry in Walsingham, one of the Catholic Movement's pre-eminent churches and parishes but in that time he had achieved much and had promised much more. The ordinand, now priest, who first met Fr Haydon at S. Stephen's House and saw the purple stole Fr Haydon always carried commented that he "was born ... only a stone's throw from some of the great Catholic shrines that my generation of priests can only catch a glimpse of through the dusty pages of the many books that now deck our book shelves. [His] down-to-earth style, his love of the Lord, and the people committed to his care, have brought the pages of those dusty books to life."[187]

---

186 Fr Patrick Allen 1955-2011.
187 Fr Robert Coates SSC.

NORMAN AIDAN BANKS

Fr Norman Aidan Banks was instituted and inducted on 6th September 2000, by Graham James, the Bishop of Norwich, in S. Mary's, Walsingham. This followed an Interregnum of 15 months. Fr Haydon's short incumbency and the suddenness of his departure and the prolonged period before the appointment of a successor meant that, despite the excellent and seasoned care of Canon Bryan Parry and other retired priests who lived in the village, it was important for the new Incumbent to recover a sense of stability and confidence in the Catholic tradition and the long-term viability of the Benefice. After four months of his incumbency, Fr Banks wrote, "In these first few months of ministering among you, I hope we can dream dreams and own a shared vision for the future, as together we seek to do God's will for the building up of the Kingdom in this special place."[188]

To this task he brought personable enthusiasm, pastoral skills honed in a taxing context, an interest and expertise in education, learning and academic ability, a keen appreciation of the significance of Walsingham and its place in the Anglo-Catholic Movement, an understanding of its history and of its importance for ecumenical relations. Yet, initially, he had not been drawn to rural ministry. When at S. Stephen's House, he had undertaken a summer vacation placement with Canon Tom Mander[189] in rural Warwickshire and "after a month of five churches discussing Harvest Evensongs and Suppers," he said that he "definitely did not see himself as a country parson."[190] To date he had spent his ministry in urban settings and

---

188 AGM Report 2000.
189 The Revd Canon Tom Mander was at that time Incumbent of Chesterton, Newbold Pacey, Moreton Morrell, Lighthorne in Warwickshire, in the Diocese of Coventry. From 1983 until his retirement in 1992, he was the Parish Priest of S. John the Baptist, Leamington Spa.
190 New Directions (ND) Interview January 2013.

although he once mused that having served in a Georgian and two Victorian churches, he might like a medieval church, he had not envisaged taking on six of them at one time.

The invitation to consider Walsingham had come unexpectedly but he accepted it with some excitement, not least because of its history and its honoured place in Anglo-Catholicism. There was also some material and practical trepidation as he was to move into a vicarage with no mains, gas or drainage, no street lighting, and "down a dirt track." He had been told, and was in no doubt, that it was to be a complex task but he soon realised that what was wanted above all else was a straight-forward parish priest with a pastoral heart.[191]

Fr Banks was born in 1954 in Wallsend on the banks of the River Tyne. As its name suggests, it marked the end of Hadrian's Wall, which stretched from there to the west coast. Wallsend was part of the Tyneside conurbation, where ship building and ship repair were still the prevailing industries and the predominant employers. His father, Frank, worked in the shipyard, in general maintenance, and his mother, Jennie, was a secretary in commercial firms and the Civil Service. His mother attended S. Luke's, Wallsend which, like most of the High-Church diocese of Newcastle, had the Parish Communion as its principal act of worship on Sundays. As a child he was fascinated and absorbed by the east window of the church. By Wilhelmina Geddes,[192] it was installed in 1922 as a memorial to those who had fallen in World War I and it depicted the scene of Christ's Crucifixion in five lancet lights. On his father's side of the family the tradition was more thoroughly and distinctly Anglo-Catholic and they worshipped at S. Peter's, Wallsend, where the liturgy and ceremonial were much more decidedly in accord with Anglo-Catholic norms. Fr John Armstrong, Rector from 1803 to 1856 was one of those

---

191 ND Interview.
192 Wilhelmina Geddes (1887-1955) was a significant member of the Irish Arts and Crafts Movement. She pioneered a revival of stained glass and a rejection of the Victorian aesthetic.

who had been influenced by the Oxford Movement. In implementing some of its ideas and doctrines, he had met some resistance from those of his parishioners who thought that he held an exalted and exaggerated view of the priesthood, as well as favouring ceremonial practices not to low-church taste. Despite a degree of opposition, he had laid down foundations upon which his successors could build. One of those was Fr Charles Osborne[193] who had been Curate to Fr Dolling[194] in S. Agatha, Landport, Portsmouth. On Fr Dolling's resignation from S. Agatha's in 1895, Fr Osborne had migrated to the north east of England having been offered the Royal Living, at the suggestion of William Gladstone, of Holy Trinity, Seghill, a small mining village about eight miles north of Newcastle upon Tyne. He subsequently moved to S. Peter's Wallsend, a plum Living in the diocese and there he prepared Fr Banks' great-grandmother and great-aunt for confirmation, providing for Fr Banks an "apostolic succession"[195] to one of the Anglo-Catholic "giants in the land." After Sunday School, Fr Banks had to report to his great-grandmother on what he had learned. She prophesied early on, "that child is destined for the cloth."[196]

The young Fr Banks enjoyed church and its social life. He was soloist at a Carol Service in S. Luke's in *Away in a Manger*, enjoyed Sunday School outings, coming second in a sand castle building competition, judged by the Curates, on Tynemouth Sands. During summer, so that they could go to the seaside, his mother attended the 8 a.m. Holy Communion on Sunday. He recalled that in those days the *Gloria* came at the end of the Service which he found very frustrating, as it delayed the start of their day out.

Fr Peter Heywood, Vicar of S. Luke's, was the first to discern a possible vocation to the ministerial priesthood in the young teenager.

---

193 Vicar from 1908-1936.
194 Fr Robert William Radcliffe Dolling (1851-1902) S. Agatha, Landport 1885-1895: S. Saviour, Poplar 1898-1902.
195 ND Interview.
196 ND Interview.

He began to introduce him to the works of Parson Woodforde[197] and Francis Kilvert,[198] eagerly discussed in the vicarage over coffee, and then to the history of the Oxford Movement, notably and significantly, directing him to Geoffrey Faber's,[199] *Oxford Apostles: A Character Study of the Oxford Movement*. First published in 1933, it was, and remains, an important contribution to the history of the Oxford Movement and was, for many, an introduction to the ideas of the Movement through the prism of the personalities of its protagonists, notably John Henry Newman but with useful insights into others, Hurrell Froude, John Keble and Dr Pusey, of the first Tractarians.

At the same time, at Wallsend Grammar School several of his teachers were practising Anglicans, some of them Lay Readers, including his History Master, Dr Frank Rogers, "a strong, formative influence."[200] Dr Rogers, a life-long Anglo-Catholic, was a talented history teacher whose enthusiasm for his subject was infectious and he was ever ambitious for his pupils. He regularly taught out of school hours and at home, principally preparing students for the Oxford and Cambridge Entrance Examinations. Dr Rogers' College happened to be Oriel, the epicentre of the Oxford Movement, and so he suggested Fr Banks apply for a place at the College. Fr Banks has "often mused that he was probably given a place at Oriel because the dons were so surprised and amused that a seventeen year old from Wallsend could speak so knowledgeably about the Tractarian Movement."[201]

On his first Sunday in Oxford, he attended Mass in Pusey House Chapel under its relatively new Principal, Canon Cheslyn Jones.[202] He

197 The Revd James Woodforde (1740-1803) *The Diary of a Country Parson*. Vicar of Weston Longville, Norfolk 1776-1803.

198 The Revd Francis Kilvert (1840-1879) began his Diary on 1 January 1870 when Curate of Clyro, Radnorshire. 1876-1877 Vicar S. Harmon, Radnorshire. 1877-1879 Vicar Bredwardine, Herefordshire.

199 Sir Geoffrey Faber (1889-1961) Publisher. Great-nephew of Fr Frederick William Faber Cong. Orat.

200 ND Interview.

201 Bp Banks in correspondence.

202 See Barry A. Orford and William Davage (Edd), Piety and Learning: The

was a noted scholar, liturgist and eccentric and, sometime Principal of Chichester Theological College. He had been much influenced by the liturgical reforms which had been introduced in the aftermath of the Second Vatican Council. Liturgical reform, Mass in the vernacular, Prayer Book Revision were in vogue. Canon Jones sought to replicate the reforms, as far as possible, in the Chapel of the Resurrection in Pusey House where a nave altar was introduced. Having been introduced after Mass, over lunch, Canon Jones, who had served his title curacy at S. Peter's, Wallsend during World War II,[203] and still kept in contact with some of the parishioners, took Fr Banks under his wing.[204]

As well as attending Mass at Pusey House and the occasional trip into the countryside, squeezed into Fr Jones' Mini, for sight-seeing and supper, Fr Banks was much involved in his College Chapel. He was Bible Clerk. His duties included saying the College's Latin Grace in Hall and answering Morning Prayer. His Chaplain was an Australian, Fr John Morgan.[205] Fr Banks also attended Christ Church Cathedral, a few yards from Oriel. The Dean was Henry Chadwick[206] and one of the Canons was John Macquarrie,[207] for whom Fr Banks regularly served at Mass. He was another "powerful and enduring

---

Principals of Pusey House 1884-2002: Essays presented to The Revd Philip Ursell [2002].
203 He served at S. Peter's from 1941 to 1943.
204 ND Interview.
205 Born in 1941. He studied at Melbourne University, graduating in 1962. He took a BA at Oxford in 1969, proceeded MA in 1973 and was awarded a DPhil in 1976. He was Acting Chaplain at Oriel in 1969 and Chaplain from 1970 to 1976. He spent the following year in the USA and the remainder of his ministry in Australia.
206 The Very Revd Prof. Henry Chadwick (1920-2008) KBE, FBA. 1959-1969 Canon of Christ Church and Regius Professor of Divinity, Oxford, 1969-1979 Dean of Christ Church, 1979-1983 Regius Professor of Divinity, Cambridge, 1987-1993 Master of Peterhouse, Cambridge. From 1969 to 1981 and from 1983-1990 he was a member of ARCIC.
207 The Revd Canon Professor John Maquarrie (1919-2007) 1970-1986 Canon of Christ Church and Lady Margaret Professor of Divinity, Oxford.

influence" on Fr Banks who found him to be "the humblest person" possessed of an "extraordinary brain" and who showed a profound "humility at the altar."[208]

Fr Banks had arrived at Oxford with an advanced sense of his vocation to the priesthood. While Fr Banks was still in the Sixth Form, Fr Peter Heywood had spoken to the Diocesan Director of Ordinands, Canon Andrew Wilson,[209] and Fr Banks had been given tea by his Diocesan Bishop, Ronald Bowlby,[210] who gave his support and encouragement. Then, his path to his first degree, graduation, theological college and ordination seemed straightforward and clearly mapped. However, there was also a pedagogic instinct and Fr Banks wanted to teach and to experience something of the "real world" and to bring that experience to any possible future priestly ministry. He was not entirely without experience in the real world. He had vacation jobs as a Council road sweeper, a Christmas postman, and a Gallery Attendant at the Ashmolean Museum in Oxford. Additionally, he served dinners to Americans who were attending summer schools at Worcester College.

Following the successful completion of his degree course, he gained a Post Graduate Certificate in Education, also in Oxford, and took up a post at the Townsend Church of England School, a comprehensive, in St Albans. What he had intended to be a year of teaching turned into three years. Although he found teaching stimulating and enjoyable, and did it longer than he had anticipated, he realised that it was not what he ought to be doing. The process towards ordination was taken up again. He attended a Selection Conference, was recommended for ministerial training and went to S. Stephen's House, returning to Oxford. This was a slight change in direction. Since 1973 he had made a strong connection with the Community and the College of

---

208 ND Interview.
209 Canon Andrew Wilson 1920-1985 Director of Ordinands and Canon Residentiary and Newcastle Cathedral 1964-1985.
210 The Rt Revd Ronald Bowlby (1926-2019) Bishop of Newcastle 1973-1980, Bishop of Southwark 1980-1991.

the Resurrection, Mirfield: he had fully expected to train for the priesthood there. At Pusey House he had met Fr Simon Holden CR[211], who became his Spiritual Director and mentor. By chance, however, he had attended a First Mass at S. Paul's, Deptford, at which Fr David Hope, then Principal of S. Stephen's House, had preached. He was so impressed that he determined that he "needed to train with and under a person with whom I was going to learn a great deal."[212] At S. Stephen's House he was also taught by Fr David Thomas[213] and Fr John Muddiman.[214] "All three helped lay the foundations for a life-long love for Scripture, Liturgy and Pastoral Outreach."[215]

He returned to Newcastle to be ordained Deacon in 1982 by Bishop Alec Graham,[216] who had succeeded Bishop Bowlby the previous year, and a year later was ordained to the priesthood. He had asked Bishop Graham to send him to an inner-city parish so that he might give something back to the kind of community from which he had come. Suitably impressed, Bishop Graham acquiesced. Consequently, Fr Banks served his title curacy with Fr Thomas Emmett, the parish priest, at Christ Church, Shieldfield. He was typical of priests in the diocese at the time, an old-fashioned High-Church, Prayer Book Catholic. His parish was an area of east Newcastle between the City Centre and Byker. It was largely a council housing estate with some streets of Victorian terraced housing. It later, after his time there, underwent redevelopment which saw the building of a number

---

211 Fr Holden 1930-2o19 He died in the 52nd year of his profession.
212 ND Interview.
213 The Rt Revd David Thomas (1942-2017) Vice Principal, S. Stephen's House 1975-1979, Principal 1982-1987, Assistant Bishop of the Church in Wales, licensed to all six Dioceses and known as 'Provincial Assistant Bishop' 2008-2017.
214 The Revd Dr John Muddiman Tutor, S. Stephen's House 1976-1983, Vice Principal 1980-1983, Fellow, Mansfield College, Oxford 1990-2012, Chaplain 1997-2012.
215 Bp Banks in correspondence.
216 The Rt Revd Andrew Alexander Kenny (Alec) Graham, Bishop of Newcastle 1981-1997.

of Halls of Residence to accommodate students at Northumbria University. When Fr Banks ministered there, it was an area of some urban deprivation. He lived in a flat in a high-rise block, partly funded by a grant from the Additional Curates' Society. Two years into his curacy, Fr Emmett had given him a degree of autonomy at S. Ann's Church, once a separate parish, on the Quayside. Fr Emmett had been persuaded to take on S. Ann's, as well as Christ Church, but did not believe that the church had a viable future. The church, although architecturally attractive, had become run-down and neglected. On first entering, Fr Banks fell in love with the building and saw its potential. After some persuasion, the Diocesan hierarchy, with Fr Emmett's blessing, decided to appoint him as Curate in Charge.

S. Ann's had been built at the expense of the City Corporation, and was completed in 1768. The architect was William Newton (1730-1798). Influenced by Robert Adam, Newton's conventional classical buildings had a Palladian elegance, typical of the late 18th century. The church was intended to serve part of the populous parish of All Saints. It became an independent parish in 1843 when a Perpetual Curacy was endowed: the patronage was exercised by the Vicar of All Saints, Newcastle. Fr Banks was given a remit to do what he wanted and thought necessary "within reason in order to see whether it could be saved from closure."[217]

To revive the fortunes of the church and the parish, Fr Banks adopted traditional, old-fashioned methods of High-Church parochial ministry. The regular celebration of Mass on weekdays as well as Sundays was introduced together with Benediction and regular Bible Studies, door-to-door visiting, maximum visibility, introducing himself, meeting people, taking full advantage of the occasional offices and organising an old-style Parish Mission, all of which raised the profile of the Church in the local community. He recruited teams of apprentices on work experience and unemployed young people to paint, decorate, repair and restore the church and its plant.

---

217 ND Interview.

Catholic discipline was central to his approach. Saints' Days were observed, the obligations of Lent were followed, feasts were appropriately kept, familial and personal rites of passage were marked sacramentally, baptism, confirmation, marriage and, also socially, additionally birthdays, anniversaries, family special occasions were observed. Anniversaries of death were kept by remembrance in Mass. The Sacrament of Confession was a regular part of the Catholic Christian life in the parish. He was, at that time, much influenced by and followed modern Roman liturgical practice post Vatican II which he first encountered at Pusey House and, later, at S. Stephen's House, Oxford. That the classical interior of S. Ann's lent itself to modern Catholic liturgical practice helped in the renewal of the parish.

He offered generous hospitality both in church and at home and gave his time to those who needed it at moments of family crisis, social dislocation, economic hardship, unemployment, delinquency; all the frustrations of everyday life in the community. He was assisted by ordinands on summer placement from Cranmer Hall, Durham, who were able to experience the life of an inner-city Catholic parish.

He also made a contribution beyond the parish boundaries. His bishop, Alec Graham, had an academic background having lectured at Worcester College, Oxford and had been Warden of Lincoln Theological College (Scholae Cancellarii). He recognised the educator and teacher in Fr Banks and appointed him to the Education Committee. Fr Banks was much influenced by Bishop Graham. "He was a prince amongst bishops … a very shy man and he certainly did not suffer fools gladly but he was quietly extremely generous … concerned for his clergy."[218] Fr Banks was not alone in admiring his idiosyncratic but compelling style of preaching. "He would mention a sermon by Lancelot Andrewes or a passage from Hooker and assumed that everyone … knew all about Lancelot Andrewes, and … was only revisiting a book by Hooker that everybody knew already … often when he preached the congregation did not quite understand what

218 ND Interview.

he said but they still felt very proud of him, and that the bishop did not condescend to them."[219] He remained at Christ Church and S. Ann's beyond the usual length of a first curacy as Fr Emmett moved to another parish, Stocksfield and Bywell, villages to the west of Newcastle in the Tyne Valley. Fr Banks agreed with Bishop Graham that his own work at S. Ann's was not yet complete and he became Priest in Charge of the united parish. Bishop Graham was prepared to appoint him to the Living but Fr Banks preferred not to be made the Incumbent, realising that, at most, he needed around three more years before moving to new pastures.

After proving the viability of S. Ann's together with Christ Church, Fr Banks spent the next decade as Vicar of S. Paul's, Cullercoats in Whitley Bay.[220] It was a seaside town centre church, well attended and supported, with a distinguished musical tradition. The congregation was largely educated, middle class, with a large number of school teachers, divided into *Daily Telegraph* or *Guardian* readers. Once a popular seaside holiday resort, and still popular with Scottish holiday-makers, it had ceded much of its clientele to Benidorm, Alicante, the Costa del Sol and Costa Brava. Much of the once thriving bed and breakfast accommodation had been converted into Nursing Homes: there were 16 in the parish. The Tyneside integrated transport system (the Tyne and Wear Metro) meant that Whitley Bay was, increasingly, a commuter town for Newcastle.

During his tenure, amidst the familiar liturgical and social life of the parish, Fr Banks continued to initiate educational projects and exercise his instinct for teaching. For three of his years there, he took some 50 people each year, of all ages, to Oxford for eight days of visits and lectures. Each year had a theme; the Medieval Church, the Reformation, the Oxford Movement. In other years there were parish

---

219 ND Interview. As he preached he would discard each completed page of the sermon onto the floor of the pulpit, or of the church. At the sermon's conclusion, he was surrounded by a sea of paper.
220 The formal dedication was S. Paul's, Cullercoats.

holidays abroad and regular pilgrimages to Walsingham. He led an annual pilgrimage to Walsingham and attended the Walsingham Youth Pilgrimage most summers, ably supported by his Curates and Mission Team.

Ten enjoyable and productive years in Whitley Bay were followed by 12 years in Walsingham as parish priest which proved a happily creative period. He volunteered that it was during the Interregnum in 1999, while sitting among the concelebrants in the parish church, that the thought had first crossed his mind wondering whether he might possibly be the next Vicar.[221] It would certainly be a very different context for ministry but he could now, despite his earlier reservations, brave becoming a country parson. He recognised that different context early in his ministry at an initial PCC "Away Day" when he said that coming from a single church in a suburban parish, the complexity of a multi-parish Benefice had come as a surprise. It was not that he had found the individual tasks were much different but that the way in which all the pieces of the Benefice jigsaw fitted together was not something with which he was familiar. The work of a parish priest was the same but the context was very different. He saw a possible danger, with such a range of responsibilities in such a diverse Benefice, together with responsibilities to pilgrims visiting S. Mary's, of being overwhelmed by activity to the detriment of pastoral engagement, the core of a parish priest's life and duty. He feared that too much had relied upon too few people and he looked forward to a more integrated and co-operative ministry.[222] Within a few years he was able to report that "the Archdeacon had described the parish as a well-oiled machine" with a much greater emphasis on lay ministry and involvement.[223] He continued the tradition of having ordinands

---

221 Bp Banks in correspondence.
222 Annual Report 2001.
223 Annual Report 2009.

from S. Stephen's House for a summer placement, Fr Richard Silk[224] in 2002 and Fr Peter Anthony[225] in 2004.

As in Whitley Bay, two of the regular features of Fr Banks' incumbency in Walsingham were the pilgrimages and parish holidays which he led and which were well supported. Early in his time as Vicar, there was a pilgrimage to Turkey to visit the Seven Churches of Revelation, which also included five days in Constantinople (Istanbul). In 2003 there was a pilgrimage to Avila, to the Shrine of S. Teresa of Avila, and another to Umbria and Rome, where at the Papal Audience "Anglican Pilgrims from Walsingham, Houghton and Barsham" were welcomed. He also attended every year the Annual Dowry of Mary Pilgrimage to the National Shrine. In 2006 another pilgrimage to Spain was made to study Carmelite Mysticism, S. Teresa of Avila and S. John of the Cross, both particular subjects of Fr Banks' interest. The following year, 2007, saw a return to both Avila and Rome. Fr Banks also spent three months on sabbatical leave during which he spent time in Italy exploring new possibilities for parish pilgrimages and holidays. In 2009 the pilgrimage destination was Padua centred on the Basilica of S. Anthony of Padua. Completed in 1310, it incorporated the church of S. Maria Mater Domini where the saint was buried in 1231. This is the Capella della Madonna Mora (the Chapel of the Dark Madonna). Relics of S. Anthony, his chin and tongue, are displayed in a gold reliquary in the Basilica. He led two pilgrimages in 2010 to see the Passion Play in Oberammergau. The pilgrimage was an important part of parish life and Fr Banks pointed out that "organising and leading such pilgrimages could not be looked on as a holiday as they involved huge amounts of work beforehand and during."[226] As Walsingham was a destination for pilgrimage nationally and internationally, it was entirely appropriate for such reciprocity.

---

224 The Revd Richard Silk Priest in Charge Devonport (S. Barnabas and Ford S. Michael) 2012-2015 Vicar from 2015.

225 The Revd Dr Peter Anthony Priest in Charge Kentish Town (S. Benedict and All Saints) 2013-2017 Vicar from 2017.

226 PCC Minutes November 2003.

Pilgrims continued to be welcomed to the Sunday Mass in Walsingham and he learned from many pilgrims of the value to them of Walsingham in the Catholic Movement. For some it seemed that Walsingham was one of the places with a Catholic tradition not compromised or, in some places, lost. The Mass on Sunday morning was for many "special because they knew what it was going to be like, that it felt safe; they felt comfortable and spiritually refreshed with it and for some it was a highlight of their year."[227] Resolutions A and B remained in place but the parish did not petition for Alternative Episcopal Oversight. Fr Banks recognised some residual tensions from the departure of a significant number of regular worshippers to the Roman Catholic Church in the village six years previously. He sensed in some a degree of nervousness and a lack of confidence that made any attempt to petition unwise and problematic. The parish acted in large part as if it was under alternative oversight but with a degree of caution and sensitivity to the Diocesan Bishop. With the agreement of the Bishop of Norwich, the ordination to the priesthood of the assistant curate, Fr John Davis, was celebrated by the Bishop of Richborough, Keith Newton, in the parish church in 2002.

Fr Banks was conscious that the Parish Church and the Shrine had different parts to play within the same domain. He well understood that the Shrine was an independent entity and charity and would have independence of action but that it was important to maintain lines of communication and mutual respect. When Fr Philip North[228] became Administrator of the Shrine in 2002, Fr Banks welcomed his appointment and told the Annual Meeting that Fr Philip had "made every effort ... to include the Benefice in his plans for the Shrine."[229] Fr Banks later suggested that there had been a perception that the Shrine was "surrounded by a wall, leading to a sense of alienation from the

227 ND Interview.
228 The Rt Revd Philip North CMP Administrator of the Shrine of Our Lady of Walsingham 2002-2008 (later Master of the Guardians) from 2015 Bishop of Burnley.
229 Annual Meeting 2002.

village."[230] Both Administrator and Vicar sought to co-operate and actively to counter that perception. That co-operation was particularly required in 2006 when torrential rain swamped Walsingham and flooded the Shrine and Abbey grounds on the day of the National Pilgrimage. A relay of Masses in S. Mary's was hastily arranged for bedraggled pilgrims and proved to be a triumph in adversity. Although there was an inevitable touch of the chaotic and an enormous amount of cleaning up, it "sent out a clear message as to how well the Parish and Shrine work together both supporting and complementing each other."[231] There was further co-operation later in the year for the celebrations to mark the 75th Anniversary of the Translation of the image from the Parish Church to the Shrine. In 2008 the 50th Anniversary of the death of Fr Patten was commemorated by the celebration of a Requiem Mass in the Shrine, followed by a procession to his grave in S. Mary's churchyard, where prayers were said.

He maintained the tradition of the Assumptiontide Lectures and invited a distinguished series of speakers on a range of Marian topics and themes.[232] He thought it fitting in 2011 to give the Lecture himself, as Vicar. The year marked the 950th Anniversary of the appearance of The Blessed Virgin Mary to the Lady Richeldis and, also the 50th Anniversary of the fire in S. Mary's. His subject was "Divine Darkness in Mary's Heart." As circumstances had it he delivered the Lecture

---

230 PCC Minutes November 2003.
231 Annual Report 2007.
232 2001 The Revd Canon Professor Dr David Brown: Pilgrimage and Imagination, 2002 Dr Ian Boxall: Mary of Ephesus and the Apocalyptic Woman, 2003 The Revd Bro Paschal SSF: Francis and Mary, 2004 Dr Luke Syson: The Madonna of the Pinks by Raphael, 2005 The Rt Revd Andrew Burnham: Our Lady of Eton and the Glory of the Eton Choir-book, 2006 The Revd Canon Nicholas Turner: Mary, Virgin Daughter of Zion, Hope of the Old Testament, 2007 The Revd Dr Geoffrey Kirk: Our Lady, Image of Woman, 2008 The Revd Canon Dr Martin Warner: The Assumption: Transitus Mariae, 2009 The Revd Canon Dr Robin Ward: The Mariology of S. Anselm, 2010 The Revd Preb. William Scott: Borrowed flesh, so gladly lent.

as the newly-appointed Bishop of Richborough before moving from Walsingham to St Albans.

His position as Vicar of Walsingham, Houghton and the Barshams involved him in the daily life of the community, the various secular institutions and with the various denominations and religious communities. These provided him with a unique perspective, and overview of how everything related and fitted together one to another. Given the diversity of traditions, as well as the different personalities in ecclesial and secular life, added to which were the shifting tectonic plates in the Church and the tensions that resulted, Walsingham could have easily become a focus for disunity and more sharply defined demarcations rather than of ecumenical convergence and rapport. Reconciliation and conciliation were attributes to be valued in a place where ecclesiologically "the colours are somehow brighter, the tunes are louder, everything has slightly more volume." The Vicar of Walsingham has a unique ministry in helping to keep conversation and dialogue open and healthy between the Roman Catholics, Orthodox and Methodist congregations in the village. As an example of this, he was delighted to be appointed an occasional preacher on the rota of the Methodist Circuit and preached in the local Methodist church.

The wider perspective was buttressed by the everyday concerns of parish and village life. Maintaining the fabric of six churches meant a constant round of repairs and refurbishment. Fr Banks was "keen and made considerable efforts to ensure repairs and improvements were made."[233] For example, S. Giles' east window was fully restored and new glazing was placed in the south porch with etched glass designed by Fr John Barnes, while S. Mary's and S. Peter's underwent major programmes of repair and restoration. In all over half a million pounds was spent on building work in the Benefice between 2000 and 2011.

As part of his commitment to village life and its material concerns, he was also Chairman or a member of the committees of several local

---

233 Brian Landale in conversation.

trusts and charitable bodies which made a significant contribution to the village and the welfare of the villagers. Early in his time as Vicar, he was surprised to find himself endorsing shooting rights over some fields owned by the Cleaves Charity. Another village trust provided uniforms for those going to the High School, while others arranged for the distribution of coal and clothing to villagers. One of the most significant trusts of which he was a member was the Cleaves Charity, which, as part of its portfolio of responsibilities, owned almshouses in the village. Fr Banks had a major role in the scheme to restore and renovate the almshouses and to build four new bungalows for older village residents. Together with generous help from the Gurney Trust, and Estate, some £1.2 million in all was raised. The time and effort involved in completing such a project contributed to the Diocesan Bishop's decision to award him a generous three months' sabbatical in Italy. He was also co-opted as a Parish Councillor: a rare, and possibly unique, affirmation from the local community. It signalled that he had "won his spurs"[234] in the village.

He also made a contribution to the diocese and to the wider church. Before his appointment to Walsingham he was an Inspector of Theological Institutions and a Selector of the Advisory Board for Ministry for those seeking ordination. It was a task that required a great deal of preparation, reading CVs, references, notes of interviews, academic assessments, reports from Diocesan Directors of Ordination for, usually, over a dozen candidates, followed by a Selection Conference, comprising individual interviews with the candidates and discussion between Selectors, lasting three or four days, to make recommendations to the respective bishops of the candidates. Only two years after his arrival in Walsingham he resigned, owing to the pressure of his other work. In 2009 he led the Norwich Diocesan Ordination Retreat at Ditchingham and preached at the Ordination Service for Deacons in the Cathedral. Although he enjoyed his role as Rural Dean between 2007 and 2011 which helped to forge links across

---

234 In conversation.

the Deanery, he regretted having ever less time for general visiting and pastoral care. He was appointed a Chaplain to HM The Queen in 2008 and served for a year as the Chaplain to the High Sheriff in 2011.

This final year as Vicar proved to be a particularly busy one. Not only was the village celebrating the 950th Anniversary of the vision of the Blessed Virgin Mary to the Lady Richeldis but also commemorating the 50th Anniversary of the devastating fire at S. Mary's. The fire was remembered by a spectacular Flower Festival and the publication of a commemorative book - *A Fire in Walsingham* - collecting the photographs, newspaper articles, and stories of the fateful night of 14th July 1961.[235] To mark the anniversary both S. Mary's and S. Peter's were rewired and new lighting schemes were installed, and work on both Vestries was completed.

His departure for the parish began with a telephone call from Lambeth Palace asking him to be prepared to see the Archbishop of Canterbury, Dr Rowan Williams.[236] The Bishop of Richborough, Keith Newton and the Bishop of Ebbsfleet, Andrew Burnham, both Provincial Episcopal Visitors, had resigned their Sees to join the newly-established Personal Ordinariate of Our Lady of Walsingham, instituted by Pope Benedict XVI for those who wished to become Roman Catholics while retaining a distinct Anglican identity. Its establishment anticipated and was irrespective of the decision yet to be made by the General Synod to allow the ordination of women to the episcopate. Fr Banks' immediate response was that his lack of driving skills and the amount of travel necessary to fulfil the requirements of a PEV were barriers to his acceptance. A more fundamental reservation, however, was that he had always seen himself as a parish priest, rooted in a particular place ministering to the people he had been called to serve. Although he had been a member of the House of Clergy in General Synod between 1990 and 2000, he had never been comfortable in the world of ecclesiastical politics and the Synodical

---

235 See Chapter 2.
236 Archbishop of Canterbury 2002-1012.

world of structures, commissions, committees and bureaucracy. Dr Williams, ever charming and persuasive, finally convinced him to accept, not least because his position in Walsingham meant that he knew most of the Anglo-Catholic wing of the Church of England. He knew them and, as importantly, he was known by them. Fr Banks was also aware from those regular contacts in Walsingham that the establishment of the Ordinariate, while a beacon of hope to some, was disturbing and disorientating to others who were still committed to a Synodical process that was not yet complete. He had sensed a degree of gloom and uncertainty, of "sheep without a shepherd."[237] He agreed to the Archbishop's request and was consecrated, with Fr Jonathan Baker[238] who had been appointed Bishop of Ebbsfleet, by Archbishop Williams in Southwark Cathedral on 16th June 2011. He was to be based in St Albans but as the house where he was to live was not available for several months, he continued to live in Walsingham and was Priest in Charge of the Benefice, insofar as his episcopal duties allowed. His last Sunday in Walsingham was 8th January 2012.

Although his duties as Bishop of Richborough cover 14 dioceses, Walsingham remains not only one of the parishes that come under his episcopal care but also the base for conferences and retreats that are organised for his Episcopal Area. There have been two Eucharistic Conferences, and there is an annual Residential Conference for curates in the Society of S. Wilfrid and S. Hilda. And, as need arises, he celebrates the Sacraments in the parish church and across the Benefice, no longer as the parish priest but as bishop.

---

237 ND Interview.
238 The Rt Revd Jonathan Baker, the Principal of Pusey House, Oxford. In 2013 he was translated to be Bishop of Fulham.

ANDREW MARK MITCHAM

Fr Andrew Mark Mitcham was inducted to the Living on 17th May 2013, following an Interregnum of almost two years. The delay was caused partly by the time it took for Bishop Banks' house to be ready in St Albans and, partly because the first round of applicants did not produce anyone whom the Patrons wished to appoint. Bishop Banks remained in the vicarage and exercised oversight of the parish, while other duties allowed, for some six months. Born in 1966 in Wisbech, Fr Mitcham was educated at Wisbech Grammar School and the University of Kent, where he read Medieval and Modern History. He was trained for the priesthood at the College of the Resurrection, Mirfield. At Leeds University he read Religious Studies. He was ordained Deacon in 1991 to serve his title at S. Edmund's, Downham Market, some 35 miles from Walsingham. He was ordained to the priesthood in the following year. In 1994 he became the Shrine Priest at Walsingham. As well as his duties in the Shrine, he joined two parish pilgrimages led by Fr Michael Rear. While Fr Mitcham was at Mirfield, Fr Rear had been his Confessor and Spiritual Director. One of the pilgrimages was to Taizé and the other to Rome and Assisi. The Taizé pilgrimage was for young people from the village, most of whom had no particular or close connection with the church. For several it was the first time that they had been abroad and, for some, their first time outside Norfolk.

At the first meeting of pilgrims, the group was singled out for a particular welcome having come from a place of pilgrimage themselves, even though the group was not entirely representative of Walsingham's reputation for reverence and devotion to Our Lady. They integrated with other young people and engaged in the worship of the community and other communal activities. One of the girls, who initially had been homesick, was in tears when it came time to leave as she wanted to stay, saying that those whom she had met had something which she did not have and that she wanted it. One of the boys celebrated his birthday there and, unobserved by the clergy, had been bought rounds of drink by his fellows. When Fr Mitcham returned to Walsingham as Vicar, he met both of them again, the boy by then a father with children in the Primary School.

Fr Mitcham joined the parish pilgrimage to Rome and Assisi as a carer for an elderly parishioner in a wheelchair who had to be pushed up and down the Seven Hills of Rome. Through his contacts in Rome Fr Rear was able to take the pilgrims to the Sistine Chapel and to the Scavi, the archeological excavations, a necropolis from Roman times, beneath S. Peter's Basilica. Fr Mitcham was able to offer Mass in the Catacombs and in the Basilica of S. Maria Maggiore.

He was the Deacon of the Parish Mass in S. Mary's after the decisive vote in General Synod the previous week that enabled the ordination of women to the priesthood. Fr Rear preached on the text, "The virgin daughter of my people is smitten with a great wound, with a very grievous blow … for both prophet and priest ply their trade through the land, and have no knowledge."[239] After Fr Rear resigned, Fr Mitcham assisted Fr Martin Warner, the Administrator of the Shrine, in running the parish during the Interregnum. He saw the significant loss of members of the parish, the effect on Mass attendance and the blow to morale among the remaining members of the congregation.

In 1996 Fr Mitcham moved to the south-east coast to take up his first incumbency as Vicar of S. John the Divine, West Worthing in the diocese of Chichester. S. John's began in 1901 as a Mission Room from the parish church of S. Botolph, Heene. The original room forms the south aisle of the present church, built in 1936-1937. An impressive, broad-base spire was added in 1966. The church was elevated to parochial status in 1955. He remained there for eight years before moving to Suffolk and the Diocese of St Edmundsbury and Ipswich, to become Rector of SS Peter and Paul, Eye. This was a very different building, one of the glories of medieval architecture

---

239 Jeremiah 14: 17-21.

in East Anglia. The church is at least 750 years old, and the site had been a place of Christian worship long before that. Its magnificent west tower is a masterpiece that gracefully dominates the village. A Rood Screen of c1450 survived the Reformation and the wrecking by the protestant iconoclasts reasonably undamaged. Still visible on the panels are 15 painted images of saints, three of them English Kings. In the 20th century Ninian Comper provided the Rood Loft with a spectacular Crucifix supported by statues of Our Lady and S. John the Beloved Disciple. He also designed a fine font cover. One of Fr Mitcham's predecessors, Canon Donald Rea (Rector 1934-1966) was a noted Anglo-Papalist, the Chairman of the Confraternity of Unity.[240] Towards the end of his ministry there, Fr Mitcham was also the Rural Dean of Hartsmere.

He was happy in his ministry there, with work still to do in the parish and deanery but he was persuaded by the Bishop of Norwich,[241] among others, to apply for the vacancy in Walsingham. Although reluctant to return to Walsingham, he did submit an application but had determined to turn down the offer if it was made. Despite one of the Patrons asking him, if appointed, to disassociate himself from the Shrine, he was offered the Living and was persuaded to accept. He did not relinquish his association with the Shrine as one of its Guardians.

Shortly before his appointment, Walsingham Primary School had become a Church School, as part of the Pilgrim Federation of Schools. Some of his predecessors had served as Governors, sometimes as Chairman, of the State School but the new Vicar had a more enhanced and significant administrative and pastoral role. It was far distant from the time when Fr Barnes struggled to gain any access to the School at all. There had been some parents who had voiced misgivings about the School's change of status and ethos; fearing it would be staffed by nuns; that their children would be indoctrinated. These

---

240 During an audience with Pope John XXIII he was given the Pope's own copy of the Breviary.
241 The Rt Revd Graham James, Bishop of Norwich 1999-2019.

phantoms did not materialise. Marshall Schaitel, the Lead Teacher at the School and Religious Education Co-ordinator for the Federation, provided encouragement and support to Fr Mitcham. They established an excellent working relationship. He was as far removed from Fr Mitcham's churchmanship as possible, as a preacher and member of the Aylsham Community Church. Marshall Schaitel recognised, however, that the Catholic tradition of the parish had to be respected. The Catholic tradition was supplemented with his encouragement of the children in leading extempore prayers during collective worship.

Fr Mitcham led collective worship each week and established a pattern of services in Church each term, rotating between S. Mary's, S. Peter's, and the Shrine Church. Many of the parents and their children, some life-long residents in Walsingham had never before entered the Shrine. Other venues in the village were also occasionally utilised. In one year the School Easter Service began with Jesus before Pilate, played by Fr Stephen Gallagher, the Shrine Priest, at the High Altar of the Shrine Church. It continued in the grounds of the Shrine with the arrest of Jesus. His trial took place in the Georgian Courtroom of the Museum. They returned to the Shrine grounds for the crucifixion at the Calvary, and the discovery of the empty tomb at the Fifteenth Station of the Cross. Jesus appeared to his disciples in the Upper Room, the Priory Refectory, and ate breakfast with them on the beach, for which the Priory pond stood in. The School Nativity Play was staged annually in S. Mary's sanctuary.

There was an annual Federation Service and one year the schools in the Federation came on pilgrimage to Walsingham where the pupils were able to show the Shrine to their fellows from other schools. The pilgrimage concluded with a service in S. Mary's. Parents and others family members attended School services. Attendance at other services, although numbers varied, saw an overall growth.

For the parish liturgy, Fr Mitcham introduced new Mass settings: *S. Thomas*, *The Gathering Mass*, and *The Coventry Gloria*. He organised a team of cantors to lead the Responsorial Psalm and, on occasion, to sing motets. He increased the number of contemporary congregational hymns that were sung at Mass and revived the parish tradition of processing to the Shrine of Our Lady after Mass, which had been in abeyance for some years, to sing the seasonal Marian Anthems. He also brought up-to-date the parish magazine that had been produced in-house and circulated among members of the congregation. He replaced it with a more professional publication, *News & Views*, a magazine paid for by advertising and annual grants from the Walsingham Parish Council, the Houghton and Barsham Parish Council, and Walsingham charities. It was a community magazine, distributed beyond the members of the congregation, delivered free of charge to every household in the Benefice. It was intended to serve the whole community and to promote community cohesion. Fr Mitcham shared the responsibility to supply monthly Christian content on a rotation basis with the Methodist Minister, the Administrator of the Anglican Shrine, the Director of the Roman Catholic Shrine, and the Orthodox Priest. Another initiative to promote community cohesion and to bring villagers and pilgrims together was an Open Garden Scheme. Proceeds were donated annually to a designated charity. The first recipient was the Walsingham Development Group.

For the first time since Fr Patten, the Vicar of the parish had a formal relationship with the Shrine. Fr Mitcham was not only a former Shrine Priest but a current Guardian. As Vicar, he was keen to forge a close working relationship with the Shrine. He had the advantage of being friends with the Administrator, Bishop Lindsay Urwin who, when Bishop of Horsham, had been Fr Mitcham's Area Bishop in the Chichester Diocese. Bishop Lindsay had also inaugurated a successful series of residential conferences at Caister, where Fr Mitcham had assisted with the liturgical arrangements. Bishop Lindsay was invited to preach in S. Mary's on a number of occasions and the hospitality was reciprocated when Fr Mitcham preached at the Shrines's Pilgrimage of Healing and Renewal, the Solemnity of the Immaculate Conception, the Pilgrimage for Priests and Deacons, and at the National Pilgrimage.

Parishioners were also encouraged to attend Sung Masses at the Shrine for mid-week Solemnities. The Shrine clergy concelebrated at the Sunday Mass in S. Mary's and altar servers were frequently those who were spending a year at the Shrine as part of the Year4God scheme. Despite these occasions of collaboration, there still remained, at least initially, among some parishioners a degree of "them and us". This dissipated over time, not least when Fr Philip Barnes was Interim Administrator and under his successor as Administrator, Fr Kevin Smith.

Without the presence of pilgrims at S. Mary's during the season, there was a regular congregation of about 50. The other churches with smaller village populations, had fewer. To sustain the work of the parishes, a stewardship campaign was sufficiently successful to secure the immediate future. From such a limited pool and with a denominationally variegated village population, it was not straightforward to recruit parish officers, servers, cleaners and all those who kept the fabric in good order, as well as to sustain organisations and events.

Fr Mitcham had to deal with the consequences of the General Synod's decision to allow the consecration of women as bishops. Although the PCC had passed Resolutions A and B following the ordination of women as priests, it and the parish priest had not petitioned under the, then, Synodical provisions for Alternative Episcopal Oversight. As all those arrangements had been repealed once it was possible to consecrate women, new provisions had been put into place. He recognised that among the congregation, and within the PCC, there were a variety of opinions. He was committed to being a focus of unity in the parish for all. Notwithstanding his personal convictions, he intended to remain committed to working with any future Bishop of Norwich or Bishop of Lynn irrespective of their sex. He would encourage their ministry in the parish to further the mission of the Church. He urged that the PCC should make its decision with regard to the Guiding Principles set out by the House of Bishops. These Principles, in part, maintained that the Church of England was fully and unequivocally committed to all orders of ministry being open equally to all, without reference to gender, and held that those whom it had duly ordained and appointed to office were true and lawful holders of the office which they occupied and thus deserved due respect and canonical obedience. Anyone who ministered within the Church of England must be prepared to acknowledge that the Church of England had reached a clear decision on the matter. Since those within the Church of England who, on grounds of theological conviction, were unable to receive the ministry of women bishops or priests continued to be within the spectrum of teaching and tradition of the Anglican Communion, the Church of England remained committed to enabling them to flourish within its life and structures. Pastoral and sacramental provision for the minority within the Church of England would be made without specifying a limit of time and in a way that maintained the highest possible degree of communion and contributed to mutual flourishing across the whole Church of England.

It was not his intention to re-open the debate on the desirability or not of the ordination of women, and the Resolution to be presented to the PCC was not to be a vote on the ordination of women as priests and bishops but it was a vote in good conscience to maintain unity in the Benefice where there were differing theological convictions in all three congregations. Nor did he intend the Resolution to be seen as a means of distancing the parish from the Church of England or from the Diocese of Norwich, but rather as a positive response to the Church's generous invitation to parishes to flourish within both the Diocese and the wider Church. In a detailed letter to his parishioners he wrote: "The passing of this Resolution is now the only way of ensuring that, in the future, the Patrons and PCC will be able to advertise for a male priest, ordained by a male bishop, to serve as Vicar here. This is clearly essential if my successor is to be acceptable to the whole worshipping community." The vote in the PCC was to be taken by a secret ballot and the wording of the Resolution was: "For the sake of the unity of our parish this PCC requests, on grounds of theological conviction set out in the statement appended to this Resolution, that arrangements be made for it in accordance with the House of Bishops' Declaration on the Ministry of Bishops and Priests." It passed in the PCC with 15 in favour, none against, three abstentions. It may have helped that the bishop who would provide oversight was the former parish priest.

That sentence from his letter turned out to be sadly prophetic. In a short time as Vicar Fr Mitcham had achieved much. He had been "a breath of fresh air ... hardworking, conscientious ... friendly."[242] However, in 2017 his ministry came to an abrupt and wretched end that cast a dark shadow over much that had gone before. He resigned and retired into private life, and was received, as a layman, into the Roman Catholic Church.

---

242 Lynette Sutton in correspondence.

HARRI ALAN McCLELLAND WILLIAMS

F'r Harri Alan McClelland Williams was licensed as Priest in Charge of the Benefice on 3rd December 2018. He was not inducted into the Living and to the office of Vicar, as the Living had been suspended to allow consideration of the addition of the village of Hempton to the Benefice. Although the Interregnum had lasted for about a year, there had been a further six months when Fr Williams' predecessor had not been able to fulfil his duties. It had been "an extraordinary year for the parishes and churches. Life was normal for

the first half and then … went into a kind of suspended animation."[243] Fr Williams' first task was the rejuvenation of parish life.

Fr Williams was born in Cardiff in 1985 and grew up in South Wales. The family moved to Newport in 1992. He was educated at

Ysgol Gymraeg Casnewydd and at Ysgol Gyfun Gwynllyw. He had not been baptised but, at the age of eight, when his parents were in the process of a divorce, he began to attend church and there he found a "sense of belonging."[244] He sang and joined the Choir of Newport Cathedral, where he became Head Chorister. Prior to University he spent a gap year in S. David's Cathedral. Here he learned much from and became good friends

---

243 Brian Landale, Vice Chairman of the PCC. Annual Report 2017.
244 The Milford Mercury Interview 8 November 2018.

with Canon Jonathan Lean[245], later Dean. Fr Williams worked as a Verger, sang in the Cathedral Choirs, and became involved in the *Friends of S. David's Cathedral*, and was its Secretary until he left the Principality for Walsingham.

He read Modern History at Balliol College, Oxford. The College Record records him as the first all Balliol baby: his parents met there in 1982 when first-year undergraduates. Both his parents read Modern History. Fr Williams played a full part in the life of the College and, in particular, the Chapel, where he was Sacristan, the first to hold that title in the College. He worked well with his Chaplain, Dr Douglas Dupree.[246] During his three years as an undergraduate, he also worshipped at Pusey House. He was a committed, devoted and popular member of the community and became the Sacristan, resident in the House and supervising the preparations for the High Mass on Sundays and Solemnities, and the daily Mass in term. He also had responsibility for the recruitment of servers and acolytes for all Masses. He persuaded several others to attend Mass, such was his evangelistic zeal. The convivial atmosphere of the House during that period of its life owed much to a series of Sacristans, all friends: Fr Philip Corbett,[247] Fr Williams and Andrew Carter.[248] One of the lasting contributions to the House was when Fr Corbett and Fr Williams descended into the crypt to help clear it before a new heating system, more archival shelves, and lavatories were installed. They uncovered and rescued a large number of portraits, photographs and artefacts abandoned by the iconoclastic zeal of a former Principal,

---

245 The Very Revd Jonathan Lean Canon of S. David's 2000-2017, Dean 2009-2017.

246 The Revd Douglas Dupree At Balliol he was Assistant Chaplain 1984-1987, Chaplain 1987-2014, Dean 2007-2014.

247 The Revd Philip Corbett Sacristan Pusey House 2005-2006, Priest Librarian and Chaplain, Pusey House 2011-2013, Priest in Charge S. Stephen, Lewisham 2013-1016, Vicar 2016-2019, Priest in Charge All Saints' Notting Hill, and S. Michael, Ladbroke Grove from 2019.

248 Andrew Carter was Sacristan 2007-2008. He is a solicitor with Addleshaw Goddard.

Canon Cheslyn Jones. Many were cleaned, repaired, restored and hung in the House. This was a significant treasure trove of Anglo-Catholic history.

Fr Williams had been accepted for training for the priesthood and was required to undertake the course at S. Michael's College, Llandaff. He graduated with a Theology degree from Cardiff University. He began a doctoral thesis on the Church in Wales and the opposition to disestablishment. It was successfully completed in 2018 when he was awarded his doctorate for his dissertation *The Life and Work of Bishop John Owen (1854-1926).*

He was ordained Deacon in 2010 to serve his title as Curate of the United Parish of Haverfordwest.[249] His training Incumbent was Fr Paul Mackness.[250] Fr Williams was ordained to the priesthood in 2011.

In 2012 he married Clare Rabjohns. She is the daughter of a distinguished priest in the Church in Wales, Fr Alan Rabjohns (who died in 2019) and his wife Gill, and the sister of Fr Ben Rabjohns, a contemporary of Fr Harri's at S. Michael's, Llandaff. There was a connection with Walsingham as Alan and Gill had met in Walsingham on separate pilgrimages in the mid-60s. He proposed to  her in 1967 on the Sunk Road in the village. Following their wedding in Swansea, they spent their honeymoon in Walsingham. During the 50 years of their marriage, they were regular pilgrims to the Shrine. Fr Rabjohns' ashes are buried in the graveyard of the parish church. Clare works as one of the editors of the 'ROOTS' Magazine and Online Resource.

Following his curacy Fr Williams was appointed Vicar of Milford Haven (S. Katharine's and S. Peter's). At the time of his appointment,

---

249 Where Fr Lean had been Vicar from 1988 to 2000.
250 The Revd Paul Mackness Vicar 2010-2014 Canon of S. David's from 2014 Archdeacon of S. David's from 2018.

he was the youngest incumbent in the Church in Wales. He arrived "fresh faced" and "some people were taken aback that someone so young could be Vicar."[251] He spent six happy years there. Having found a rather quiet church, with no children at Mass, he applied his energies to increasing the number in the congregation, which by the time he left had doubled to some 120. He paid particular attention to ministry among the young of the parish. He started a Sunday School, initially with one child, which grew as numbers of adults with young children in the congregation increased. He formed a Youth Group which he was told "would not work," but it grew to some 25 young people by the time he left. Such was its success and the commitment of the young that several of the older members, who had been among the original recruits, took over the running of it when he left. He said that it succeeded because the young felt valued, they had found a home in the same way that he had when he was young. He took a group to the Youth Pilgrimage at Walsingham every summer and raised funds to cover the costs. For some it was the only holiday they would have in the year. He was clear that "you cannot invest in the building if you are not prepared to invest in people." This work among young people also benefited the older members of the congregation, giving them a new lease of life.

He also developed links with the schools in the parish, the Meads Primary School, Milford Haven Junior School and Milford Haven School. He was instrumental in re-opening the Mount Community Centre in an area of social and economic deprivation to encourage the acquisition of skills and the fostering of friendships and mutual support. Nor did he neglect the priestly round of visits, ministering to the sick and housebound, and births, marriages and deaths; as well as pastoral encounters at times of difficulty. Over £200,000 was raised for the church building and hall and to restore the World War I Memorial Chapel, an asset for the community as well as the church. It is unsurprising that these achievements in a relatively short space of

---

251 The Milford Mercury op cit.

time meant that at the time of his departure for Walsingham he was described as the "best known face" in Milford Haven.[252]

He has quickly established himself in Walsingham and the surrounding villages. Beyond the parish boundaries he is also making a valuable contribution to the wider church and in the Catholic Movement.

---

252 The Milford Mercury.

For more than the hundred years surveyed in these pages, Walsingham has witnessed to the Catholic Faith. It has remained at its heart a Norfolk village but with an acknowledged and special place beyond its parochial boundaries in the Catholic Movement and in the Church of England. It has not been untroubled by the turmoil of the times; nor has it been without controversy in its recent past, as in its more distant past, as the 100 years covered by this book bear witness. Fr Alan Roe had to succeed one of the major figures of Anglo-Catholic history and his sudden death. Fr Roe's own ill-health meant that his successor, Fr John Barnes, had to re-establish a pattern of ministry and worship. Fr Michael Rear's succession was the most straightforward of this century of the parish's life but his leaving was the most traumatic, as he had to face the most serious fissure in Anglo-Catholicism and the wider church in the 20th century. Fr Haydon entered into a depleted and fractured inheritance. His tenure was abrupt, cut short by personal circumstances. Although Fr Norman Banks' leaving Walsingham was to episcopal office, a tribute to the parish as to his own qualities, it necessitated a period for the parish of suspended animation until Fr Andrew Mitcham's appointment. His leaving was also abrupt and occluded his previous work. Fr Harri Williams came to a wounded parish and one conscious of its history and its more recent past, of good and ill. He brought his skills and determination to meet the challenges.

If Walsingham has reflected the highs and lows of life as it has been lived these hundred years, it has been constant in its witness to God, incarnate in his Son, Jesus Christ, and the working of the Holy Spirit; and its dedication to God's own Mother, Our Lady of Walsingham, *Ora pro nobis.*

APPENDIX I

Walsingham Assumptiontide Lectures

1979   The Revd Dr Eric Mascall: The Centrality of Mary
1980   The Revd Dr Edward Yarnold SJ: The Assumption
1981   The Revd Professor Dr John Macquarrie: The Glorious
       Assumption
1982   The Revd Dr Donald Allchin: The Joy of Creation
1983   The Revd Canon Cheslyn Jones: Our Lady and Oxford
       Movement Thought
1984   The Revd Dr David Hope: Our Lady in the Liturgy
1985   The Rt Revd Dr Graham Leonard: The Body of Christ
1986   Pamela Tudor-Craig, Lady Wedgwood: The Virgin
       Mary as Seat of Wisdom
1987   The Revd Canon Dr Roy Porter: Mary: The Old
       Testament Background
1988   The Revd Dr Jeremy Sheehy: Immaculate? What does it
       mean to be 'without original sin'?
1989   The Revd Michael Rear: Marx or Mary
1990   The Revd Philip Steer: Singing the Dormition from the
       Festal Menaion
1991   The Revd Dr Gordon Wakefield: Mary, Mysticism and
       Human Need
1992   Dr Eamon Duffy: *Title not known*
1993   Dr Nigel Yates: Loss and Recovery: The Blessed Virgin
       Mary in Anglican Thought and Practice 1600-1900
1994   Dr Julian Litten: Folklore Traditions of Our Lady
1995   The Very Revd Stephen Platten: Saints, Shrines and
       Pilgrimages
1996   The Revd Peter Allen SM: *Title not known*
1997   The Revd Dr Robert Hannaford: Our Lady, Hope of
       Christians

1998   Dean Leif Norrgärd: Marian Devotion and Reflections of the Role of Mary in the Scandinavian Churches

1999   The Revd Alan Williams SM: Aspects of Pilgrimage

2000   The Revd Canon Bruce Ruddock: "Full of Grace and Hope" Mary and Anglican-Roman-Catholic relations today

2001   The Revd Canon Professor Dr David Brown: Pilgrimage and Imagination

2002   Dr Ian Boxall: Mary of Ephesus and the Apocalyptic Woman

2003   The Revd Bro Paschal SSF: Francis and Mary

2004   Dr Luke Syson: The Madonna of the Pinks by Raphael

2005   The Rt Revd Andrew Burnham: Our Lady of Eton and the Glory of the Eton Choir-book

2006   The Revd Canon Nicholas Turner: Mary, Virgin Daughter of Zion, Hope of the Old Testament

2007   The Revd Dr Geoffrey Kirk: Our Lady, Image of Woman

2008   The Revd Canon Dr Martin Warner: The Assumption: Transitus Mariae

2009   The Revd Canon Dr Robin Ward: The Mariology of S. Anselm

2010   The Revd Preb. William Scott: Borrowed flesh, so gladly lent

2011   The Rt Revd Norman Banks: Divine Darkness in Mary's Heart

2012   The Rt Revd Jonathan Baker: Our Lady, Queen of Heaven

2013   The Rt Revd Dr John Hind: Behold your mother: Mary, the Church and the Christian believer today

2014   Dr Colin Podmore: Blessed Virgin: Mary and the Anglican Tradition

2015   The Revd Dr Peter Anthony: The Transfiguration and Our Lady: some patristic perspectives

APPENDIX II

Parish Priests of Walsingham before 1921

(as recorded by Fr Patten in his Short Guide to S. Mary's Church)

1494	James Ive
15 --	William Wettstow
1524	John Dyx
1532	John Thorp
1564-1585	Henry Corker
1585-1598	Samuel Stallon
1598-1615	William Knowles
1615-1619	William Simpson
1619-1638	Herbert Warde
1647	Thomas Displine
1662	James Watts
1662-1670	Edmund Turner
1670-1672	Charles Robotham
1672-1680	Henry Pitts
1680-1681	Thomas Bliford
1681-1717	Thomas Clithero
1717-1723	Joshua Thompson
1723-1729	John King
1729-1755	Henry Roberts
1755-1774	Morgan Powell
1774-1807	Michael Bridges
1807-1834	James Lee-Warner
1834-1859	Henry James Lee-Warner
1860-1870	Septimus Henry Lee-Warner
1870-1871	Frederic William Kent
1871-1882	William Martin
1882-1888	George Ratcliffe Woodward
1888-1904	Henry Arthur Wansbrough
1904-1920	Edgar Lee Reeves

APPENDIX III

Administrators of the Shrine of Our Lady of Walsingham

1931-1958	The Revd Alfred Hope Patten
1958-1968	The Revd Canon Colin Stephenson
1968-1972	The Revd Charles Smith
1973-1981	The Revd Alan Carefull
1981-1986	The Revd Christopher Colven
1987-1993	The Revd Roy Fellows
1993-2002	The Revd Martin Warner
2002-2008	The Revd Philip North
2009-2015	The Rt Revd Lindsay Urwin
2016	The Revd Philip Barnes (Interim)
2016-	The Revd Kevin Smith

INDEX

A

Allchin, Canon Donald - 64, 135
Anglican-Methodist Covenant/Reunion - 66
Anglican-Roman Catholic International Commission - 33, 78, 79, 81, 107
Anglo-Catholicism - 11, 13, 14, 18, 20, 21, 23, 30, 32, 42, 43, 51, 52, 54, 56, 60, 64, 66, 71, 78, 80, 81, 82, 84, 86, 87, 88, 89, 92, 93, 95, 102, 103, 104, 105, 106, 120, 123, 131, 134, 137
Assumptiontide Lecture - 63, 76, 100, 1166, 135

B

Baggley, Fr John - 92
Baker, The Rt Revd Jonathan - 37, 120, 136
Balliol College, Oxford - 130
Banks, The Rt Revd Norman Aidan - 41, 103-120
Barnes, Fr John Edgar - 37, 46, 51-67
Barnes, Fr Philip - 126, 139
Benson, Fr Richard Meux - 94
Bishop, Canon David - 65
Blake, Naomi - 65
Book of Common Prayer (BCP) - 7, 15, 54
Bowlby, The Rt Revd Ronald - 108, 109
Brighton - 13, 98
Burnham, The Rt Revd Andrew - 116, 119, 136

C

Carefull, Fr Alan - 37, 48, 52, 53, 55, 59, 60, 64, 139
Carlyle, Abbot Aelred - 13, 23, 26
Carter, Andrew - 130

Great Walsingham, S. Peter - 21, 46, 55,
Gurney, John - 53, 73
Guthrie, Edna - 93, 94

H

Haydon, Fr Keith Frank Michael - 6, 27, 84, 86-102
Hoey CR, Fr Augustine - 63
Hope, Fr David - 64, 109, 135
Holy Cross, Cromer St - 14
Holy House, Walsingham - 14, 25, 40, 57, 66
Houghton, S. Giles - 13, 16, 46, 54, 55, 63, 68, 74, 77, 80, 86, 114, 117, 125
Howe, Betty - 10, 21, 25, 31, 38
Howard, Graham - 10, 37, 41, 149
Huddleston CR, Most Revd Trevor - 91

I

J

James, The Rt Revd Graham - 103,123
John XXIII, Pope - 31, 43, 123
Jones, Canon Cheslyn - 64, 106, 130, 135
Julian, Revd Mother - 61

K

Kelham Theological College - 30, 92
Kemp, The Rt Revd Eric - 43
King, The Rt Revd Edward - 92
King, Major Patrick - 60, 80, 95
Kray, Reginald (Reggie) - 93

Kray, Ronald (Ronnie) - 93

L

Landale, Brian - 10, 56, 117, 129
Larkworthy, Peter - 57
Lean, The Very Revd Jonathan - 130
Lee-Warner, Philip (and family) - 54
Leonard, The Rt Revd Graham - 43, 64, 135
Lichfield Theological College - 14, 69
Lingwood, Fr Derrick - 20
Little Walsingham, S. Mary - 15, 20, 21, 32, 34-37, 41, 46, 47, 49, 54-57, 62, 64, 65, 73, 77, 82, 85-87, 91, 95-101, 103, 113, 116, 117, 119, 122, 124-126
London, Bishop of - 64

M

Mackness, Fr Paul - 131
Mackonochie, Fr Alexander Heriot - 88
Macquarrie, The Revd Prof Dr John - 107, 135
Mascall, Fr Eric - 63, 135
Mitcham, Andrew Mark - 121-128, 134

N

Newman, S. John Henry - 14, 83, 85, 106
Newton, Rt Revd Keith - 115, 119
North, The Rt Revd Philip - 115, 139

O

Ordinariate of Our Lady of Walsingham - 119, 120
Ordination of Women - 65, 79, 80, 82, 86, 95, 119, 122, 126, 127

Oriel College, Oxford - 14, 52
Oxford Movement - 14, 16, 17, 24, 66, 81, 105, 106, 112

P

Palumbo, Peter (Lord) - 65
Patten, Fr Alfred Hope - 5, 11-29, 139
Paul VI, Pope - 32, 43, 70
Pilgrim Federation of Schools - 123
Preston, Fr Frederick - 90
Pusey House, Oxford - 10, 11, 64, 106, 107, 109, 111, 120, 130

Q

R

Rabjohns, Fr Alan - 131
Rabjohns, Fr Ben - 131
Rabjohns, Clare (See Williams) - 131
Rabjohns, Gill - 131
Rea. The Revd Canon Donald - 123
Rear, Catherine (Cathy) - 69
Rear, Fr Michael John - 6, 11, 12, 14, 27, 30, 31, 37, 48-50, 68-85, 95, 100, 101, 121, 122, 134, 135
Roe, Fr Alan Arthur - 30-50, 134
Roe, Heather - 31, 48-50

S

S. Asaph Cathedral - 53, 54, 59
S. Asaph with Tremeirchion - 53
S. Barnabas, Pimlico - 14, 89, 90, 114
S. Botolph, Heene - 122
S. Chad's College, Durham - 51